Hunting Trophy Whitetails

Previous Buckmasters Books

Jackie Bushman's Top 50 Whitetail Tactics

Jackie Bushman's Big Buck Strategies

Hunting Trophy Deer: The Best of *Buckmasters Whitetail Magazine*

Hunting Trophy Whitetails

Tales of Record-Book Bucks

Edited by Darren Brown

Introduction by Jackie Bushman

The Lyons Press
Guilford, Connecticut
An imprint of The Globe Pequot Press

Copyright © 2002 by Buckmasters

Illustrations by Chris Armstrong

All rights reserved. No part of this book may be reproduced or transmitted in any form by any means, electronic or mechanical, including photocopying and recording, or by any information storage and retrieval system, except as may be expressly permitted by the 1976 Copyright Act or in writing from the publisher. Requests for permission should be addressed to The Globe Pequot Press, P.O. Box 480, Guilford, CT 06437.

Printed in the United States of America

10 9 8 7 6 5 4 3 2 1

Library of Congress Cataloging-in-Publication Data

Hunting trophy whitetails : tales of record-book bucks taken by the readers of the nation's most popular deer-hunting magazine / introduction by Jackie Bushman.
    p. cm.
 ISBN 1-58574-744-0 (hc : alk. paper)
 1. White-tailed deer hunting. I. Bushman, Jackie.
SK301 .H86 2002
799.2'7652—dc21
                                            2002015274

ISBN 1-58574-744-0

Contents

Introduction vii
1. The Culvert Buck   1
2. Scouting Pays!   7
3. The Dream Buck   12
4. Shed Hunting for Trophy Bucks   17
5. The Dream Year   22
6. Rainy Day Surprise   29
7. Old Crooked Horns   34
8. Lucky Thirteen   39
9. Two Records in Two Years   43
10. What Would Dad Do?   49
11. Ohio Buck Raises the Bar for Handgunners   54
12. Sportswoman's Paradise   59
13. It Pays to Have Friends   65
14. Family Affair   70
15. Bruiser from Bull Creek   74
16. Pee Dee Buck is No Pee Wee   79
17. Trapper John's Buck   86
18. On a String: The BTR's No. 1 Typical by Recurve   90
19. Cyclone   94
20. The Bean Field Buck   99
21. A Sandhills Stalk   104
22. South Carolina Hunter Finds Nugget in Nibblet Country   108
23. The Patient Hunter   114
24. The Schoolyard Buck   119
25. The Swamp Buck   125
26. Second Chance in Saskatchewan   131

CONTENTS

27. Family Farm Bonanza 138
28. Monster of Muscatatuck 142
29. Home Field Advantage 148
30. Missouri 19-Pointer: Worth the Wait 152
31. Land of the Giants 156

Introduction

Unlike other sports, hunting has no arena, no grandstand, no victory circle. When hunters perform extraordinary feats, as they often do, there is no cheering crowd to applaud. That is as it should be. Hunting is not a contest. It is a means of harvesting food. More than anything, it is a lifestyle of enjoyment that continually builds respect for the great outdoors.

Anyone can get lucky on a hunt and shoot a trophy, and we all know entertaining stories of those who have, but to repeatedly track and harvest record book deer is the mark of a master hunter.

In athletics, the rule of thumb is that you don't improve by playing opponents at your level or below—you learn more and improve your ability by getting on the playing field with those who are better than you. We can't put you in the treestand with great hunters, but we can make you feel like you've been there by sharing their stories and their secrets with you. That's what this book is all about. It tells the stories of many of the hunters who have repeatedly taken deer that qualified for entry in "Buckmasters Whitetail Trophy Records."

In some of these stories you can almost smell the early morning mist in the woods and hear the rainfall in the trees. It's a book that will teach you new things about hunting from some of the world's top hunters. But it's also the closest thing you'll

INTRODUCTION

find to a hunting trip into the woods from the comfort of your recliner.

    We hope you enjoy *Hunting Trophy Whitetails*. And, the next time you go hunting, remember to take a friend or family member who might not otherwise get to go.

— Jackie Bushman

1

The Culvert Buck

Hunter: Richard Blauser
BTR Score: 147⅛
Date Taken: Oct. 1, 1995
Typical; Compound Bow

You won't hear Richard Blauser complain about not having sole access to thousands of acres of trophy-managed private lands. Blauser consistently takes large bucks on public land and in areas others don't think to hunt—all in the heavily-hunted woodlands of western Pennsylvania, where bucks usually only make it to a year and a half of age. He's hunted here all his life, spending a great deal of time scouting, and most importantly, he

Veteran bowhunter Richard Blauser has taken an impressive number of trophies from the hard-hunted woods of western Pennsylvania over the years, including the 147 1/8 (typical) BTR-scored buck in this story.

knows that big bucks sometimes turn up in the oddest places. His four Pennsylvania-harvested Buckmasters record-book bucks are ample proof that his method of hunting has worked exceedingly well.

Here's the story of how he took one of these rare Pennsylvania bucks back in the mid-1990s in Allegheny County. He first spotted this buck during the archery season of 1994 while scouting a new area when the sun flashed off the buck's rack as it hid in a timber slashing. He quickly found a convenient spot for a treestand and came back the next morning to hunt. Just after daybreak he saw the buck at about a hundred yards as it headed into a creek bottom. A half-hour later, a doe came up from the same creek and walked right under Blauser's stand. After watch-

THE CULVERT BUCK

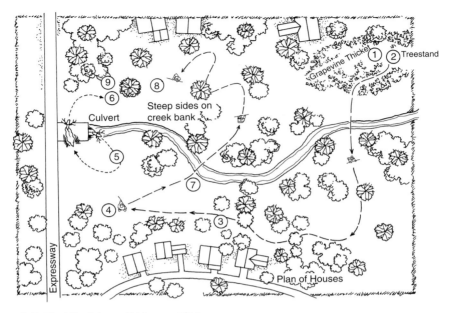

1) Rattled Buck in on Friday morning
2) Left tree stand on Monday because of dogs
3) Hunted toward Expressway
4) Saw deer come out of culvert and shot
5) Hit deer
6) Last place to see deer
7) Ran up creek to get shot if deer came up creek bottom
8) Crossed creek and looked for deer or blood trail
9) Found deer laying dead

ing the doe pass, he turned to check her trail and found himself staring right into the eyes of his buck at about 30 feet. It was gone in a flash.

The next morning he saw him again, walking 30 yards below in thick brush, which didn't allow for a clean shot. Despite further efforts, that was the last Blauser saw of the buck for the rest of the season.

In September of the following year, a friend of Blauser's mentioned seeing a monstrous buck settled in on a hillside overlooking an expressway in a wide suburban area. This was only about a mile and a half from where he had seen the big buck the previous year, and it quickly became apparent that it was the same one he'd been chasing. He already had permission to hunt the property across the road from the buck's location, and as he knew the area pretty well it wasn't difficult to place a ladder stand in a spot that would afford a good shot at anything moving through.

The next morning, he was on the stand before daybreak. As it began to get light, Blauser rattled some antlers a few times then sat quietly to watch the results. The rut was on and almost instantly he made out a large deer coming up a trail near the stand, but it was still too dark to tell if it was a buck or a doe. As it closed the distance to only 20 feet or so, he saw the now-familiar rack. If the buck continued down the path it would pass just three feet behind the tree where the stand was located.

Blauser froze in position to let the buck pass, but after about two minutes without seeing him appear on the other side of the tree, he slowly turned his head to where he'd last seen it. The buck, with some sixth sense warning, was standing stock still 10 feet away, staring straight up at him. It swung around and with a couple of leaps was gone again.

After spending the weekend hunting small game with his son, who had just started hunting, Blauser was again sitting in his stand well before daylight on Monday morning, determined to finally get the best of this cagey buck. Several deer passed through around 8 a.m., including a small 8-pointer, but not the big buck.

Soon after, he heard a loud noise that was approaching quickly, and he turned to follow it, only to see three dogs burst into the open, scouring the area before passing on.

He figured that would ruin everything in the immediate vicinity for a while, so he climbed down from the stand and started walking an old pipeline toward the expressway. It was proving too noisy to ease quietly along, as the oak leaves that blanketed the ground crunched unavoidably with every step, so he stopped to scan the cover in front of him. He was just 100 yards from the expressway and 70 yards from a small creek that ran under the road. The culvert that carried the flow of the creek under the road was around seven feet in diameter and 100 yards long. As Blauser carefully searched the creek bottom, the big buck that had bested him twice popped right out of the culvert and walked up the hill in his direction. When the deer turned broadside to the creek, Blauser drew his bow back, judging the range at 45 to 50 yards, a distance at which he regularly practiced and at which he felt comfortable shooting. With the noise the buck was making moving through the leaves, Blauser felt sure he wouldn't hear the sound of the string. He held just in front of the slowly moving buck and saw the arrow bury itself in the front end of the deer as it bolted away.

The buck ran back toward the culvert but veered above it and back down the slope on the other side of the creek before disappearing. He seemed to be moving parallel to the creek, and Blauser immediately moved to get in position near a sharp bend ahead of the buck. This would give him a clear 20-yard shot if the buck continued running up the creek—if he could get into position in time. He got to the spot he wanted and waited, but no deer came. As he also had a clear view of the hillside opposite the creek, he decided the deer must have doubled back toward the culvert.

He crossed the creek and slowly started working back down, expecting to jump the buck at any moment. When he was within 20 yards or so of where he'd last seen the buck, he spotted the white belly among the oak leaves in a small ravine. It was too large to dress and drag without help so he tagged it and came back as quickly as possible with a friend. Closer examination showed that the arrow had gone right through the heart.

The buck measured 147 1/8 inches in the Buckmasters scoring system.

2
Scouting Pays!

Hunter: James Stovall
BTR Score: 203 6/8
Date Taken: Sept. 25, 1999
Irregular; Compound Bow

When I heard that the Green Swamp WMA was going to take in another 38,000 acres of basically virgin territory that had not been hunted for 13 years, I put my name in the hat for one of the 54 permits to be granted for two different bowhunts. Fortunately, I was drawn.

I began scouting the land after ordering and obtaining topo maps and aerial photos of the area in June. The number and

James Stovall's amazing bow-bagged buck scored 203⅝ (irregular) and received Buckmasters' Golden Laurel Citation in 2000.

sizes of the buck rubs immediately impressed me. Some were the size of my lower leg, and I heard others claim they found rubs the size of their thighs. I don't doubt it. After weeks of scouting, I had located several shooter bucks (four points on at least one side to be legal), but none that I wanted to hunt. I was seeking a buck for the records, and I knew that property was capable of producing book-class animals.

Five days before the Sept. 25 opener, I was scouting and found four huge tracks. Knowing that the bucks were still in bachelor groups, I figured these were four good bucks, probably traveling together. I started tracking the deer the best I could, but the terrain was incredibly tough. The deer had wandered through palmetto flats interlaced with cypress hammocks and tightly woven thickets of myrtle bushes and gawberries. I was finally able to slip inside the bucks' core area by pure stubbornness and persistence. Sure, I lost the tracks many times, but I was able to circle and zigzag until I rediscovered them.

I had gone maybe 1,000 yards when I found myself staring at a buck the size of . . . Well, there was about 200 inches of antler atop the feeding deer 40 yards in front of me. And he had no idea I was there.

I watched him for nearly two minutes through my binoculars. I tried my best to count his points, but all I counted was 17 (of the rack's 26) because he kept moving his head. Finally, he grew uneasy and slowly moved off in a stiff-legged walk. He wasn't sure what he saw, but he knew something was out of place.

The buck walked around a cypress pond and stood over there for close to 20 minutes. During that time, he shook like a dog after getting a bath, scratched his back with one of his drop tines, and he groomed his neck and face with his rear hoof. Other than that, he stood like a statue—staring back in my direction. My arms were so tired of holding up my field glasses that I had to use a scrub oak limb as a prop. He finally slipped back into a thick tangle of palmettos and gawberries. After mentally choosing the best spot for a treestand, I also slipped out of the area.

A tropical depression out in the Gulf of Mexico was supposed to hit shore the following morning. I went back anyway to hang my stand and trim some limbs, knowing that Mother Nature would wash away any trace of my presence. As I slipped into the area, I spooked four dandy shooters, including the big buck, right under my chosen tree. Three hours after leaving the woods, I was dealing with mixed emotions. I was excited that there were four nice bucks in my area, but now I would be hunting one that knew he was being pursued.

The next week, I could not focus at work. I was losing sleep, and I was not eating right. This buck had literally taken over my life. I was determined to sit all day on Saturday, opening day, because I would not be able to do it on Sunday.

I was already dressed before the alarm sounded at 3 a.m. I reached the WMA's gate at 4:00, an hour before it would open. No one else had arrived yet. I was pumped. I wanted to get to my stand well before daylight to allow the woods to settle. It was also a 30-minute walk to my stand, and I didn't want to rush and work up a sweat. But I need not have worried. The full moon enabled me to slip quietly into the setup.

Daylight broke right after three deer walked under my tree at a mere 10 steps. The deer seemed to be following the trail I'd laid with my drag rag. One of them had a fairly high and wide rack, but he was not the big irregular buck. The rest of the morning was mostly uneventful.

Around 4 p.m., high winds, a light rain, and haunting dark clouds filled the sky as a storm pushed its way up the state from the Caribbean. With winds gusting at more than 30 miles per hour, the storm passed quickly. At 6:10, I made another visual sweep of the area, and I did a double take back to the northeast. "There he is!"

I'm not sure if I said that aloud. I quickly glassed him and confirmed that he was indeed the huge irregular buck. Even at 150 yards, I could see his distinct rack with my naked eye. He was feeding in my direction until an 8-pointer walked out and started feeding parallel to my stand. He was a great buck in his own right, but a dwarf compared to the one I wanted. The respectful, smaller buck eventually fed uphill, leaving the big guy back in the thicker cover.

Finally, at around 6:40, my buck stepped into the clear. He looked uphill at the other buck, 200 yards distant, then he twitched his tail and began feeding in the same direction. I knew I needed to get in front of his path, and I knew exactly which path he was going to take.

I held my bow in my teeth, stepped off my stand, and slipped down the stick ladder. Upon reaching the ground, I glassed the deer once again. All was calm in his world, while mine was reaching an excitement level understood only by a bowhunter. I crawled in a semicircle about 150 yards to get in front of him, through palmettos and scrub oaks. When I could not risk another move, I slowly nocked an arrow and rose to my feet. Nearly 15 long minutes passed before he reached bow range.

Watching such a buck that close was not easy. I was as nervous as a long-tailed cat in a room full of rocking chairs, but I also was confident in the shot that was about to present itself. When the buck put his head down to feed, I slowly drew and sent an arrow toward my unsuspecting target. "SMACK!" The arrow dropped the buck with a hit to his spine. A quick follow-up shot behind the last rib finished him.

I ran back to my stand to retrieve my video camera. My face and my voice betrayed my excitement.

After taping the "walk-up" (I couldn't film myself taking the shot), I set up the camera, walked around in front and put my hands on the deer for the very first time. It was a long 13 hours in the tree, but the reward was well worth the effort.

The deer weighed 150 pounds, and he was only 3½ years old. Not only is he the No. 1 irregular bow buck for Florida in the BTR, but he also is tops in the Pope & Young Club's non-typical velvet category.

3

The Dream Buck

By Dan Infalt

Hunter: Brad Kuhnert
BTR Score: 190 2/8
Date Taken: Nov. 23, 1997
Semi-Irregular; Rifle

Although Brad Kuhnert of Fall Creek, Wisconsin, had taken more than a dozen mature whitetails off public lands during his hunting career, the hard-core hunter longed for a world-class buck, the kind most folks only see in magazines. Dreams of such a trophy continued to haunt him until the day he saw a magazine pin-up feeding along the edge of a clear-cut. He knew instantly that deer was the trophy for which he'd always been searching.

THE DREAM BUCK

Brad Kuhnert's dream buck was harvested after extensive scouting trips allowed him to be in the right place at the right time.

Kuhnert played a game of cat and mouse with the monster whitetail during most of Wisconsin's bow season. Whenever their paths crossed, the buck was always just out of range, or an ethical shot was not possible. The hunter began to look forward to the nine-day gun deer season, but it came and went with no further contact. He passed up several nice bucks, always hoping to get a glimpse of the bruiser with which he was obsessed.

This buck was different. Bagging all of his previous bucks was child's play compared to hunting for him, he thought.

The season's ending only signaled the beginning of Kuhnert's preparations for the 1994 season. He started scouting every chance he got, searching for bigger-than-usual tracks, large rubs, any signs that might offer clues to the whereabouts of the magnificent animal's hideout. Eventually, he found an area that looked good. There was very little evidence of deer activity, but the few signs present were left by a very large buck.

After more exploring, Brad also found an adjacent bedding area. He tied a ribbon at the intersection of two trails.

The following spring, Kuhnert found another good-looking spot about 200 yards from the junction of the trails. He also located a tree overlooking both spots, one from 100 yards away, the other from a distance of 300 yards. He would be ready when the season started.

As devoted to hunting whitetails as Brad is, he is even more devoted to his family. Since he'd promised his wife Mary and daughters Heather and Hope that he would build them a house, he was not about to renege because bow season had opened. But he was mentally reserving time for the gun season. He tried hard to get all of his work done in time for opening day.

When it came, he was in his stand an hour before daylight. He saw two small bucks. The next day, he counted only one little buck and two does. Then he had to work for a couple of days before resuming the vigil.

On the fifth morning of the short season, it was still dark when Brad reached his tree. He heard a couple of deer moving just south of his stand, so he stood motionless and they passed. Afterward, he quietly climbed up and settled into his stand.

A few hours later, he spotted the buck about 300 yards away in some thick brush. The next five minutes were long and tense as Brad waited for a clear shot. Finally, the monster stepped into a clearing—it was Brad's only chance at a shot.

With the crack of the rifle, the buck jumped up into the air. But he took only a couple of steps into the brush. The deer was just standing there, looking around him. Brad wondered how he could have missed.

Without answering himself, he again took careful aim and squeezed the trigger. The buck's response was to take two more steps, stop and continue looking. Was this buck invincible?

Thinking the buck was about to step out of sight, a frustrated Brad stared through his scope a third time. The only clear shot was to its spine, but he would have to take it. The dream buck was just one step away from disappearing. But suddenly the wind picked up, the trees began swaying and Brad was having a difficult time preventing his crosshairs from dancing. With a super effort, he just held the crosshairs on the buck until they seemed to "lock in." Then he touched off another round.

The buck disappeared that time.

Did he go down? wondered Brad, peering through his binoculars.

He was disappointed to see a deer walking away from where the buck had been standing, but his excitement was renewed when he saw that it was a doe. He watched as she took a few steps; stopped to look behind her; took a few more steps; looked back again; then ran. Thankfully, nothing followed her.

Brad waited 20 minutes before getting down from the tree. He wanted to be ready if the buck showed itself again. Finally, however, he couldn't stand it. He went to the place where he thought he'd last seen the dream buck. He looked around; saw nothing. He made some small circles, too, but still found nothing.

"Concentrate," he told himself.

That's when he remembered a small pine tree next to which the buck was standing. He looked around for the tree and spotted it 50 yards away. When he got up next to it, he noticed the ribbon he'd tied to the brush the previous spring, when he'd found the area. The buck was lying less than 10 yards from the ribbon.

The buck scored 190⅞ (Semi-Irregular) in the Buckmasters scoring system.

After admiring the buck and congratulating himself on his scouting, Brad began to fit the pieces of the puzzle together. He figures the buck and doe must have been the two deer he heard in the pre-dawn darkness. They had bedded down just before dawn, and the buck must have risen around 9:30 to stretch his legs.

When he went down again—with the help of two bullets—it must have spooked the doe, forcing her to rise and flee.

Turns out, Brad's first shot was true—right behind the shoulder. He also discovered where the second bullet hit some brush and deflected. His third shot was also right on the money, breaking the buck's back and dropping him in his tracks.

Brad's buck scores a whopping 190⅞ semi-irregular in BTR's centerfire rifle category.

4

Shed Hunting for Trophy Bucks

Hunter: Lance Jacob
BTR Score: 191 6/8
Date Taken: Nov. 6, 2000
Semi-Irregular; Compound Bow

Lance Jacob's intense scouting paid huge dividends when he harvested a buck that scored 191⅝ BTR points a couple of years ago in Kansas. Lance says he spends about twice as much time hunting sheds and securing permission to hunt than he does actually hunting, and it gives him an excellent feel for where big bucks are in his home state. He uses this knowledge to study areas in more detail and work out feeding and bedding areas and

Lance Jacob worked hard to learn the habits of this buck over several seasons before he finally had a chance to take him with a compound bow. The buck scored a whopping 191% (semi-irregular) in the BTR record book.

travel routes where he knows big bucks will be. He doesn't worry much about cover or attractor scents or odor control, but instead relies on knowing which locations to hunt with the prevailing wind to keep himself downwind of any deer in the area.

While scouting in 1998, Lance found the shed antlers of a particularly large buck and began to search out scrapes, rubs, and other sign in the area. In 1999, he'd hunted the area hard, working from two stands and frequenting the area often in less than optimum conditions as his obsession with the buck of his dreams grew. His only glimpse of the buck that season was all too brief—ended by the loud and untimely squeak of his treestand as he shifted his weight. The buck was gone in an instant, but Lance had recognized the impressive shape of his rack from the sheds he had at home.

The following spring he again found the buck's shed antlers nearby. With some time to reflect away from hunting season, Lance decided to remove one of his stands and resolved to only hunt the area when conditions were perfect. He also was determined to let the buck stay more comfortable and settled by not working the area so hard.

In November of 2000, Lance was again in position to have a try at the buck during the rut. A large bedding area was located on one side of the stand he had left in place and the timber funneled down to additional feeding and bedding areas. It was obvious that a lot of deer had been moving through the vicinity. A cornfield ran parallel to the side of the small drainage he was hunting and a good deal of transition cover was mixed in with the timber. The stand was located on the east side of the drainage and the wind was out of the northwest, leaving him downwind of any deer using the trail.

Lance had been hunting most of the day in another area where he'd found some other large sheds that spring. With the rut going strong, he was doing a lot of rattling but to no avail. Around 3:00 p.m. he decided conditions were right for another try at the buck he'd been tracking for several seasons now, and he quietly climbed into his Loggy Bayou treestand. He saw a lot of small bucks chasing does, but nothing of enough size to tempt him. As he had his rattle box with him, he spent some time playing with the little bucks, letting them wander off and then luring them back with a quick rattle.

A little after 5:00, and ten minutes or so from the last time he'd rattled, a doe appeared to the north of his stand, feeding

Lance poses with the collection of sheds that have led him to several trophy-caliber bucks. The shed hunting he does in the spring plays a large role in how and where he hunts in the fall.

along the drainage. He knew there was a good chance a buck would be following and he waited and watched. Suddenly, a giant buck appeared, and Lance immediately recognized the antlers—his antlers—as it headed right for the doe.

There was no time to do anything but pick up his bow and shoot. Just seconds after spotting the buck, Lance loosed an arrow that hit him in the right shoulder blade. Lance saw the arrow penetrate but stop after just 4 or 5 inches. It wasn't a perfect shot, but Lance thought that the Muzzy broadhead had gone in far enough to make a good kill.

The deer ran for about 40 yards and then stood still. With darkness closing in, there was nothing Lance could do. Any move might spook the buck, sending it miles away with little blood to follow. Eventually, the buck walked another 15 yards or so and stopped again. With each breath Lance saw him wag his tail like he was having trouble breathing, so he did the only thing he could do; he waited until he had the cover of darkness and then snuck down from his tree as quietly as possible and returned to his truck.

It was driving him crazy to be so close to his goal after all that time, but experience told him that patience was his only option. He got cleaned up and went to work on the third shift—there was no trouble staying awake on the job that night, although Lance didn't get much work done—and returned as soon as he could in the morning.

He found the spot where the buck had been standing and then saw his arrow broken off. He began to worry that the hit wasn't good enough to anchor the buck, but all fear evaporated when he spotted it stone-dead just 10 yards from where he'd last seen it the night before and less than 80 yards from where he'd found its sheds the previous spring.

5

The Dream Year

**Hunter: Mark Armstrong
BTR Score: 190
Date Taken: Nov. 17, 2001
Irregular; Compound Bow**

My story begins following a long dry spell of hard hunting every season for the previous five years. My quest to arrow another book deer finally ended on Nov. 16, when I arrowed a buck that would qualify for the record books. The 10-point beauty was a near twin to the buck I shot in 1995, which scored in the mid-150s.

My brother and I had been camping down by Winterset earlier in the week and we decided to move the camper to the southwest corner of the state on Thursday, as the wind was gust-

Mark Armstrong with the first of the three bow-harvested record-book bucks he took in one remarkable season.

ing at more than 30 mph. We figured it would be a good day to change locations since the hunting would be tough.

I dropped Mike off at his house and headed for the campground. I had the camper set up by 2:30 and decided to hit the woods for a few hours before going home to spend the evening with my wife. That plan was wonderfully foiled by the 10-pointer.

He came in following a doe and presented a broadside shot at 12 yards. I put a perfect "X" through his heart and watched him go down. Almost immediately a smaller buck came down the trail to pursue the doe. Then to my continued amazement, I heard a third buck grunting repeatedly.

When I saw this buck, I almost had a heart attack. He was even bigger than the buck I had just dropped. I tried to nock another arrow, but the buck took off after the doe. I hit the grunt call, but he just kicked into a higher gear, showing me his backside as he went.

Even though I didn't get a shot at that bigger buck, I had a real trophy on the ground and was more than happy about it. Boy, am I glad I went hunting that evening instead of going directly home. My wonderful wife, Stacy, understands when it's hunting season, and she knows as well as I do that you can't get a buck sitting on the couch.

I had put my landowner tag on the 10-pointer and still had another tag. Visions of that bigger deer kept haunting me.

THE BIG ONE

The next morning, Mike joined me as planned. After a quick look at my buck and listening to him tell me I was a no-good so-and-so, we headed for the timber with high hopes. We shared the anticipation of new hunting territory (okay, so I had hunted it once), and it was getting close to the peak of the rut.

There wasn't much activity in the morning, so we worked on our treestands between the morning and evening hunts. That afternoon I headed back to my stand where I shot the 10-pointer. Mike was set up a few hundred yards away on the end of a funnel.

I had been in the stand for only a few minutes when a doe appeared, coming down the same trail as the evening before. Following her was the biggest buck I had ever seen! The right main beam was unbelievably long, and the deer had more points than I could or cared to count.

I remember telling myself, "Quit breathing so hard!"

The buck started down the trail after the doe but then stopped, went back up the trail and proceeded to make a fresh scrape at the base of a cedar tree.

After finishing the scrape, the buck returned to his pursuit of the doe, which had by this time wandered off the trail and away from me. I remember thinking that I would wait until he came to an opening I had made. I would grunt and stop him, then shoot.

Everything worked according to plan except for one thing. The buck was really keyed up and jumped the string when I shot. I hit him, but the shot was at the back of the ribcage, dead center in the middle of the body. The buck took off, and I got the shakes.

I sat down, watched, listened and waited—and shook.

It had seemed to me that the buck hadn't left the brush he'd run into, so I waited until full dark to get down and look at my arrow. It didn't look good, as it had exited through the intestines, so I decided to go get Mike without even attempting to track the buck. I knew if I had any chance of recovering him, I needed to be cautious and not push him.

Mike, of course, accused me of putting him on a nonproductive stand as we tiptoed out of the timber with plans to look for the buck in the morning.

That night seemed like it lasted a week. Morning finally arrived.

Stacy drove down the next morning to hunt with Mike and me. We had decided to go ahead and hunt in the early morning and then attempt to track my buck. Even though I still had two bonus doe tags to fill, the morning dragged on. At about 10:30 I went to get Stacy. We decided to stop by the neighbor's house, Terry, and tell him we'd be tracking a deer just in case he had someone hunting his property. Terry asked if he could join in the search, and we were glad for the extra help.

He then asked if the buck was a tall 8-pointer that would probably score in the 150s. I told him I thought it was more like a 12-pointer—or bigger!

We got to my treestand and I was encouraged to find a nice trail of bright red blood. I thought, "We're going to find him any time." Then the trail just stopped!

The second buck he took, a 16-pointer, proved to be the largest of the group.

We could see where the buck had lain down and just quit bleeding. The four of us combed the area, coming up empty.

We were about to give up when I said to Terry, "If I bumped him when I got down from my stand he might have gone across the bean field to the timber on the other side. What do you think?"

Terry, being familiar with that side of the timber, sent me down a trail he knew the deer used quite a bit; he went to the next ridge to the north.

I headed down the trail, which appeared to be leading to the bottom of the Grand Canyon. I remember thinking that I could sure use a miracle right then. I was just about to the bottom of the canyon when I saw what appeared to be a huge deer head sticking out from under a fallen tree.

"No way," I said aloud. I knelt down, trying to focus and believe what I was seeing. It really was my buck. I took off at a dead run, hollering at the top of my lungs, "I found him! I found him! Thank you, God!"

The 16-point non-typical will score in the 190s Boone and Crockett and has a 22-inch inside spread.

That was an incredible 24 hours—two record-book bucks from the same treestand, and I even got to enjoy the moment with my wife and some good friends.

UNBELIEVABLE . . . NUMBER THREE

The above story would be enough to make anybody's season one to cherish forever, but there's more. I still had the late season to hunt. I had a half dozen new arrows, got in some extra practice, and was ready to head out again.

Wednesday, Dec. 20 arrived with temperatures in the upper teens—a heat wave! I headed out to my stand—yes, the same one—and stayed there until 4 p.m. I saw an owl and a mangy coyote but no deer. I moved to another stand at the edge of a bean field to see what was coming out to feed. At about 4:45 a few does came out but quickly went back in the timber.

As darkness approached the wind started to blow and I was getting cold. I was just about ready to call it a day when I looked up to see a deer coming out on the other side of the field. It didn't take long to see he was a buck.

As he got to the middle of the field I realized his current course would not bring him within bow range. I dug deep in my pockets and finally located my grunt call. I blew it as loud as I could and the buck stopped in his tracks.

I hit the call one more time and he started to trot my way. He got to within 20 yards, and I had to mouth-grunt to stop him.

I didn't hesitate and watched my arrow strike home.

Buck number three was just icing on the cake.

This time I was confident of the hit and I began to trail him almost right away. I went about 100 yards when I jumped a deer. Not knowing if it was him, I decided to call it a night and come back with help in the morning.

The blood trail was still visible the next morning, despite the 30 to 40 mph winds that had blown all night. We had to literally crawl through the evergreens to stay on the blood trail but found the buck about 50 yards beyond where I had quit tracking him.

He turned out to be an 8-pointer with a broken brow tine. He scored about 133, capping a truly incredible Iowa bow season. Adding the three deer together, I was fortunate to take 491⅝ inches of antler in just 33 days.

Of course, now the inevitable question comes up, "How do you top a season like that?"

Well, I don't know that I ever will. I'm just thankful I had the season I did—and of course I can always try like heck to have another.

6

Rainy Day Surprise

Hunter: Dale R. Larson
BTR Score: 264 5/8
Date Taken: Nov. 7, 1998
Irregular; Compound Bow

As I was listening to the raindrops play their rhythm on the fallen leaves, I noticed the flick of a tail and glimpsed a deer's antler. The buck was about 90 yards distant, walking along a brushy fence line—traveling perpendicular and away from my position. My view of the thicket was obscured by scattered trees and brush, making it impossible to maintain visual contact.

I retrieved my grunt call from my rain gear and blew a couple of low, tending grunts. At that moment, the buck was

Expert bowhunter Dale Larson with "Dagger," one of the most impressive whitetail bucks ever taken.

entering a dogwood thicket. I couldn't see his response, so I called again with more gusto, but I still couldn't see him. Thinking that any more volume might blow him out of the country, I decided to call it quits. As I was putting the call away inside my rain suit, I caught sight of movement 25 yards in front of me. I saw immediately that it was "Dagger," and he was coming on a dead run.

A LITTLE BACKGROUND

I was introduced to archery at the early age of 8, although I did not start hunting whitetails until 12 years later. After 10 years of it, I began targeting only mature bucks.

Bowhunting has been a major part of my life. My wife, Connie, is also an experienced bowhunter, and my stepson, Matt, is fast becoming one. Our devotion to whitetails is a yearlong endeavor. We manage for quality, do a lot of off-season scouting, engage in shed hunting, recreational viewing of wildlife, and actual hunting. In fact, one of the keys to our success is year-round involvement.

The majority of our hunting area is tallgrass prairie, wooded drainages, and small cultivated fields. Our woodlands consist of several species of hard- and softwoods that spread up the drainages and out into the grasslands like fingers on your hand. The small amount of cropland is spread between the upland and bottomland, giving the land a mosaic pattern with an abundance of edge habitat.

We'd come to call one of the best bucks inhabiting the tract "Dagger" because of a drop tine on his left main beam that grew down and backward. We first saw him when he was 3½ years old, when he was otherwise a mainframe 10-pointer. He continued to carry the drop tine throughout his lifetime. The next year, his rack carried only nine points, but went back to 10 before eventually growing a 12-point frame.

I had wanted to film Dagger's antler development during the summer of 1998, but my star was playing hard to get. I had some bad thoughts of Dagger succumbing to hemorrhagic disease, which had plagued the local deer herd. I was having a hard time staying optimistic, although we found his previous year's sheds, but at least we knew he had survived that long.

The first sighting of Dagger last year occurred when Connie and I were going to vote. It was almost dark when my wife spotted a large deer in the pasture. I tried to identify the deer through my binoculars, but with the light conditions and quick sighting, I wasn't sure. What I could see was that the deer had a huge typical frame with a long drop tine on the left beam. If it wasn't Dagger, he was still a keeper.

The second time I saw him was with my stepson, Matt. It was also near dark, about one mile from the previous sighting. Just as before, the encounter was brief, but encouraging. He was still alive!

BACK TO THE HUNT

Although I knew from previous calling experiences to be ready for action, I was not prepared for the deer's fast and aggressive response. The buck ran directly under my stand and stopped. He stood there turning his head first one way, then another, trying to locate the vocal intruder. Standing 12 feet below me was Dagger—the buck of a lifetime—and my bow was still hanging on its hanger.

While I was pondering my next move, Dagger started walking toward the edge to look downhill. Thinking it was "now or never," I put my hand in the bow sling, removed the weapon from the hanger, stepped back, and drew—all in one slow and deliberate motion. I fully expected to see him looking up at me when I got settled in my stance, but he had continued to slowly walk away from me. I positioned my 20-yard pin behind his right front shoulder and let instinct take over, sending the arrow to its mark. At the impact, Dagger lunged forward and ran downhill and out of sight. I could hear his retreat for a few seconds, and then all was quiet.

After waiting about 30 minutes, I headed back to meet my hunting partner, Perry, at the truck. We both arrived at about the same time. I told him that I had shot Dagger and I did not think he went very far. We drove back to the house to pick up flashlights, my wife, and stepson. Because of the light rain, we decided to start the tracking job sooner rather than later. Upon reaching the site of the shot, we found the lower half of my arrow lying beyond where the deer had been standing. The blood trail started immediately, and his staggering tracks were easy to follow. We had gone between 70 and 80 yards when we saw his antlers in the flashlight's beam.

This magnificent animal was something to behold. He had fallen in such a way that his long drop tine held up his head. At this position, you could see all the kickers, stickers, and his huge typical frame. Everyone there had dreamt of harvesting this deer, and most had enjoyed (or not enjoyed) an opportunity. We were all amazed at his size and did nothing but admire him for quite some time.

Dagger scored an amazing 264⅝ in the Buckmasters scoring system. He was 6½ years old.

7

Old Crooked Horns

**Hunter: Jeff Novak
BTR Score: 184 5/8
Date Taken: Dec. 7, 1998
Irregular; Rifle**

Six days into the 1998 rifle season, I was aiming at a buck I had not seen since opening day in 1995. I thought the big guy was dead, or at least so old that he couldn't grow a good rack anymore.

Three years earlier, my dad (Roger) and I got up at the crack of dawn one day and drove around for a couple of hours, hoping to see some bucks. We didn't see much that morning, so we stopped to ask our neighbor, Frank, if he wanted to go hunt-

Jeff Novak's fine buck scored 184⅝ (irregular).

ing for awhile. We wanted to have an extra guy to walk out some ditches, and Frank was glad to come along.

After running a couple of evergreen patches behind his house, Frank bagged a doe. But he still wanted to keep hunting with us. We wanted to hunt a section northeast of there, so I dropped Frank and dad off at the north road and I went to block at the south. Frank was on one side of the creek without a gun, and dad was on the other as they started to walk my way.

Dad said that when he made it to the half-mile line, he jumped a huge buck below a pond dam that took off through the evergreens. The buck ran right at Frank and, when he got there, Frank began hollering—turning the buck in my direction. In fact, most of the deer that were jumped headed my way.

A little later, I saw four bucks on the side of the creek. I could tell they were all bucks, but it was too brushy to determine how big they were. As I was looking them over, I turned to see two of the biggest bucks I had ever seen cross the road about 200 yards from me. One was a huge 7×6 with the P-3s on each side angling in a couple of inches from the rest of the rack. The other buck had an extremely wide set of antlers with five points on each side. Both the deer had very long tines.

I emptied my gun, but my heart was pounding so hard that I could hardly hold the gun straight. The bucks ran across a short wheat field and faded off, unharmed, into the timber.

I stood there for a couple of seconds and kicked myself in the butt, because I knew that I had just missed the chance of a lifetime. I took off to find dad and Frank. When I did, we decided to set up on the bucks and let them come by us, but they never did. That's when I started walking the creek to where dad was taking a stand next to some big round bales.

When I jumped the two bucks again, they split. One went toward dad, but "Crooked Horns" (the nickname we gave the buck with the pair of crooked tines) slipped past us. The other buck wasn't so lucky. Dad got the 5×5.

From that point forward, I wanted "Crooked Horns" so bad that I could taste it. I even set out to find his sheds. I found both sides from 1994 and 1995—all in the same section, the parcel he had come out of the first time we saw him. For the next two years, however, he was nowhere to be found.

A few people claimed to have seen him outside of deer season, but he apparently knew where to hide when the season's first gun was fired, and we couldn't figure out where that was. We hunted every place we thought he might be, and we still couldn't find him again.

In 1998, I had pretty much given up on "Crooked Horns." I classified him, like too many others, as the one that got away. During the first few days of the season, we saw a lot of bucks. But I was holding out for one a little bigger.

On the season's fifth day, it rained. After walking around in the wet stuff all day, the scope on my .243 had gotten moisture in it and I didn't know it. The next morning, I went down to dad's and picked him up to go hunting. Shortly afterward, we saw two nice bucks run into his section. When I picked up my gun to look

Jeff poses with his buck and the buck's sheds from two earlier years.

them over, I couldn't see through the scope. A seal had gone back and moisture was blurring the optics. I grabbed dad's .270 and took aim but, by that time, they were too far to shoot.

The two bucks made it to the timber, and I sent dad in behind them. I took his gun and he took mine, because I thought I would have a better chance of getting a shot blocking at the opposite end. He agreed, and away we went.

Dad said that when he got to the half-mile line, he jumped a monster. The buck took off, then jumped the fence and went back into the timber. At the south end, deer started coming out everywhere. I didn't know which way to turn. Finally, I spotted a buck. He was a smaller 4×4 that I let pass. Then, all of a sudden, out from behind a row of big round bales came a giant. I instantly knew this was the one. When they are this big, you don't have to make a decision; you just know.

As he jumped the fence, I hit him right in the side. I wasn't going to let him get away this time. He stumbled and went down, and as I reloaded, he got back up and headed for some CRP land. Knowing that deer can be very hard to track in the thick brambles, I shot him again—not wanting him to make it that far. He went down for good that time.

As I walked up to him, I couldn't believe my eyes! This was the buck that I had been trying to get for the last four years. It was "Crooked Horns!" Only this year he had broken off one of his crooked tines. He'd also grown a drop tine on that same side.

8

Lucky Thirteen

Hunter: Mark Verble
BTR Score: 163
Date Taken: Nov. 8, 1995
Semi-Irregular; Compound Bow

Mark Verble was attempting to harvest his 13th antlered buck in his 13th year of hunting in Orange County, Indiana in 1995, but superstitions didn't affect him when he took a trophy-caliber buck that season, one of three bow-killed bucks he's put in the "Buckmasters Whitetail Trophy Records."

The archery season opened on October first and he hunted hard the first three weeks of the season, hunting almost every day. He saw several small bucks, but nothing he wanted to

Mark Verble took this beautiful buck with a compound bow. It scored 163 (semi-irregular) in the BTR system, and is one of several Mark's put in the record book.

take, particularly that early in the season before the upcoming rut made even the most careful buck lose its natural caution.

Back trouble kept him out of the woods for a couple of weeks, but with the rut peaking during the second week of November, nothing was going to stop him from taking to the woods. On November 8th he was set up in a treestand about 18 feet off the ground on his father-in-law's farm. It was a promising area, set in a small grove of white oaks on a hillside overlooking a densely covered creek bottom. The grove was located about halfway up a hillside, with an alfalfa field about a quarter-mile away on top of the hill. From earlier scouting trips he knew that there were numerous rubs along the creek bottom and scrapes on the hillside, and the deer had obviously been using a trail that ran along a fence going to and from the field. A perfect spot to target deer as they moved to and from feeding areas early and late in the day.

Mark set his stand about 20 yards back from the fence, using a rangefinder to make sure he would be shooting at a comfortable range with his compound bow. He also placed a little Tink's #69 about 20 yards downwind from the stand to attract and hold any buck that ambled by. He was excited, as the deer had obviously been using the oaks a good deal. "It looked like hogs had gone through the trees."

The stand was on the east side of the oaks, and Mark made sure to only use it with a wind from the west or north. Although he now uses Scent-Lok clothing, back in '95 he was just careful to work the wind to his advantage and washed his hunting clothes frequently.

At about 4:45 that evening, he began to rattle. Two small 8-pointers appeared from a low ditch and walked down the fencerow in front of him. The second buck was definitely shootable and it was difficult to hold back, but he passed on these bucks, knowing that something bigger must be in the area.

He didn't have to wait long. Five minutes later another buck appeared. There was no doubt about this one. He was headed down the same trail the first two bucks had used. As the buck came closer, Mark drew his bow. But the deer, guided by the instinct for caution that had seen him through many hunting seasons, turned right and circled around behind the stand. Fighting back panic, Mark waited to see what the buck would do. Luck was with him, as the buck turned and walked directly beneath the stand. At just four yards, Mark loosed his arrow. The buck ran back toward the bottomland. After thirty minutes or so, Mark climbed down and followed. He knew it had been a solid hit and he wasn't too worried about pushing the buck.

There was blood on the ground and he easily followed the trail for 150 yards or so. Suddenly, the resting buck jumped up before him and bounded off for another 50 yards before collapsing. This time for good.

The buck dressed out at 170 pounds and had a BTR score of 163 in the semi-irregular category, with an inside spread of 19¼ inches and 16 scoreable points on an 11-point frame.

Thirteen was Mark's new lucky number.

9

Two Records in Two Years

Hunter: Dan Rederick
BTR Scores: 177 6/8, 198 2/8
Dates Taken: Nov. 5, 1997, Oct. 12, 1998
Semi-Irregular; Compound Bow
Irregular; Compound Bow

THE FIRST RECORD BUCK

During a day of harvesting corn in October 1997, deer hunting took on a whole new meaning for me. Without any warning, right in front of me jumped the biggest buck I had ever seen. One

Dan Rederick poses with two record-book deer he took with a compound bow in consecutive years in South Dakota. The buck on the left scored 177⅝ (semi-irregular) and the one on the right totaled 198⅞ (irregular).

moment he was there; the next, he had disappeared over the hill. I sat there for awhile, questioning what I'd just witnessed. I could not believe what I had just seen, and I could not wait to tell my dad.

When my father finally showed up at the field, I told him about the monster buck. He did not believe me, saying, "Oh, you're just pulling my leg." That is when I thought, "Fine! I'll just have to prove it to you."

While combining, I started to look seriously at the lay of the land. There were about 400 acres of corn, three stock dams, sloughs, and a small grove of trees. I decided to put a stand in the trees closest to where the buck had been bedding.

I sat in the stand a couple of hours for five mornings. Since we were still combining, that was all the time I had. The first couple of mornings I saw the monster buck up in the same area. He was traveling with a dozen does and a smaller buck. It was very hard to see them because it was very dark when they appeared.

I figured I had him pegged after the second day, so going back to the same stand on the third morning was an exciting prospect. To my dismay, however, I saw nothing. I did not see the monster buck again for more than two weeks. I was almost ready to call it quits, ready to accept that he had moved out of the area and into the sloughs and timber.

With that in mind, I put up another stand about three-quarters of a mile from the first sighting. This one was near a stock dam and a grove of trees. I could see all around the area.

I arrived at my new stand on the morning of Nov. 5 about a half-hour before daylight. I brought my decoy with me, which was sweetened with a doe-in-heat scent. I had never used a decoy before, but I thought I'd give it a try.

I had only been in the stand about 10 minutes when I heard a buck grunt. Then another one grunted. I knew there were two different bucks. It finally started to get light enough for me to see with my binoculars. I spotted the group of deer about 200 yards distant. The big buck was with the does, a smaller buck, and another big one. I couldn't believe bucks were together at that time of year.

I started using my grunt call, then bleating, but nothing happened.

I continued to watch the deer. The bucks would roll their heads toward each other, but they never fought. As morning broke, I began to wonder what I could do to get close enough for a shot. I decided to wait and let the deer make the first move. They finally did, but not toward me. The monster buck started to move away from the rest of the herd and away from me. I had to watch this monster buck go over the hill.

The other deer started moving downwind of me, so I started grunting and bleating to see what would happen. After only a few seconds, I noticed the does mingling around about 40 yards from my stand. Then I heard a cracking of branches and turned to see the little buck and the other big buck. A couple of short bleats grabbed the attention of the little buck. He responded by walking right up to the decoy.

The big buck stayed in the trees for a long time before he made his way to the decoy and past my stand. I wasn't even thinking about shooting this big buck at the time because of the monster buck I had been watching for so long. But when this buck came within five yards of the decoy and stopped to look at it, I realized for the first time how big this guy actually was. One brow tine, for example, grew 15⅝ inches tall.

I slowly drew my bow and released the arrow. It passed right through, and the buck darted. As I watched him run away, I actually thought I had missed. His legs finally buckled, however, and he fell after running 100 yards. After crawling down from my stand, I ran over to where he went down and I couldn't believe how big this buck was. This is also when I realized how big the other one—the buck I'd jumped that day in the corn—must have been.

I hunted for that monster during rifle season, but I never did see him. After the season was over, he reappeared. I looked for that deer in 1998, too, but I never saw him again.

I'm glad I saw the monster first because, when this big buck came by, all I could think about was the bigger one. It actually helped stop the jitters of seeing a 177⅞ (BTR) buck on the hoof.

BESTING THE BEST

When the 1998 bowhunting season opened, I was hoping for the monster buck that I had seen the previous year. I started scouting areas really early in the year, and I saw good sign. I told a friend of mine, Tim, who lives to hunt, to get a bow license so we could hunt together. He agreed. I put up a stand near a cornfield and gravel pit. I told Tim that we could share the stand because I knew there was a nice buck in the area.

When the season started, I didn't have much time to hunt because of farming. I told Tim to go ahead and sit in the stand. He later told me that he had seen lots of does and some little bucks, but nothing big. I told him that, sooner or later, one of us would get a nice buck out of that stand.

On Oct. 12, my wife had a meeting in town, and I was with her that day. When we returned home around 4 p.m., I told her that I was going to go out and sit in the stand for awhile to see what I could see. I knew it was going to be late when I got there, but I thought I would try anyway. When I climbed into the stand, there was only about 45 minutes of daylight remaining. Only a minute or two had passed when some people in a pickup drove through the area. I thought to myself, "Boy, this night is finished. There isn't going to be anything coming out of the trees to feed now."

Five minutes later, however, I heard something within the trees. I couldn't believe it. Here came a deer—a buck whose rack looked very different. I soon realized that it was an irregular monster (but not THE monster I'd been hunting). He was on a fast walk.

I tried, but I couldn't get him to stop, so I decided to draw my bow. I put the pin on the buck and let the arrow fly. It entered behind the back rib and exited at the sternum, and the deer bolted.

Everything happened so fast, I had no idea of the buck's true size.

It was getting dark, so I decided to get down from my stand and to look at the arrow. It had passed right through and stuck in the ground. After examining the blood, I ran to my truck and called Tim and some other friends from town to see if they would come and help me look for the deer. When they arrived, we waited for about 15 minutes before we started tracking.

We looked for about a half-hour before we decided to go home for the night. The next morning, we found where the buck had fallen about 100 yards from where I had shot him. We had apparently spooked him during our nighttime search, and I was worried that he had gone a long distance. We decided to spread out and walk along the corn and in the grass. I sent Rob, another friend, down along the creek. An hour had passed before I heard Rob yelling, "Here he is! He's by the creek!"

We all ran over to where Rob was to see the buck. We could not believe it. He was a huge 13×9, and the rack would tape out at 198⅝ BTR—even bigger than my 1997 buck's headgear.

10
What Would Dad Do?

Hunter: Arnold Holmes
BTR Score: 156 3/8
Date Taken: Nov. 1993
Typical; Rifle

Arnold Holmes lives in some of the finest big game country in North America. Growing up on a farm in eastern Saskatchewan, he shot his first deer, a 5×4, at the tender age of nine with a .22 automatic and has been hunting hard ever since. He's become a much sought after outfitter for many species of big game, which leaves him little time to hunt whitetails these days. But he still has six 140- to 150-class bucks recorded in the

Arnold Holmes has been hunting in the Canadian wilds since he was a kid. *(photo by Gene Bidlespacher)*

Buckmasters record book from earlier days alone after whitetails. He learned most of what he knows about big game from his father, an excellent shot and an experienced woodsman. When he's faced with a tough decision like the one in this story, Arnold still asks himself: What would Dad do in this situation? As you will see, it paid big dividends.

One of Arnold's favorite hunts for whitetail occurred while he was still working long hours at a local mill in the late 1980s. Each payday, he'd have enough money for a box of shells with which to practice his shooting and to hunt with. And every spare minute was spent in the outdoors. He first caught sight of

Although his outfitting business now keeps him from hunting whitetails as often as he used to, Arnold Holmes still managed to put half a dozen 150-class trophies in the BTR record book, including these beauties. *(photos by Gene Bidlespacher)*

this particular whitetail buck while calling in moose. The rack he caught a glimpse of impressed him and he quickly resolved to hunt only this buck when the general deer season opened. The moose hunt had taken place near a low, swampy area, and with careful study he was able to discern the whitetail's tracks in the soft ground. One of the buck's hind legs toed out slightly when it walked, so he could easily recognize the track every time he came across it.

The season finally came, and he spent a week and a half after this deer, following its tracks and learning the areas where it liked to bed and where its rubs and scrapes were located. The deer was clever, though, managing to stay out of sight during this time. Arnold saw a lot of other respectable bucks, but held off in anticipation of getting a chance at just this buck.

The forests were of poplar and spruce with low swamps and grassy sloughs and draws and creeks—thick cover mixed with small openings. Finally, new snow fell and he could easily track his buck again. Rutting season was going strong and the buck was covering a lot of ground. Arnold eventually picked up fresh tracks after a four-mile walk into the depths of the forest. There were several rub lines and scrapes in this area and it soon became obvious that the buck was checking and refreshing them as he moved along. Arnold began to quietly follow the fresh tracks through the soft snow.

The buck was traveling east, with the wind in his face, so as long as Arnold was able to move quietly, he figured that he wouldn't spook the buck because he was well downwind. With just an hour to go before dark, he got a fix on where the buck was heading and followed for another half-mile or better. He suddenly came upon a spot where the buck had broken into a trot and then made a few big jumps. Arnold stopped to assess the situation. He knew he hadn't spooked the buck because the wind was still from the east and the soft snow muffled every sound, but the buck must have sensed that something was amiss. It had no reason to run, but now that it had, Arnold had to make a quick decision that would either successfully end his long hunt or leave him a long, cold walk home empty-handed. Experience and instinct told him that the buck would be turning back to his home turf to seek the security of his usual bedding areas.

There was no time to think further. Arnold swiftly turned and ran back to a slough he had passed earlier that ran north to south, which might give him a glimpse of the buck if it had, indeed, turned toward home. If the educated guess had worked, the buck would have to cross the open ground of the slough to reach his home ground to the west. Sure enough, the deer had circled, and suddenly he broke into the open across the slough at just over a hundred yards. Arnold dropped to one knee and centered the open sight on his much-used Browning lever action rifle on the running buck. He swung the rifle with the moving deer and squeezed the trigger without thinking. He was an excellent shot and had practiced extensively on just this kind of moving target. The buck piled up in a heap and Arnold had his 150-class buck after a long, but rewarding hunt. His father would have been proud.

11

Ohio Buck Raises the Bar for Handgunners

*By Sallie Schneider Sauber
(as told by her father)*

**Hunter: Joseph Schneider
BTR Score: 203 2/8
Date Taken: Nov. 30, 1998
Irregular; Pistol**

It was a hot day in late August and I was finishing up my mowing for the year. Sitting on a John Deere all afternoon amongst the ragweed and orchard grass is usually my least favorite task, but this time was different.

Joseph Schneider is used to seeing impressive bucks, but this monster, which he took with a handgun, is certainly one for the books.

The blade had caught a rock, so I looked behind me to make sure another pin had not been sheared. Everything seemed to be okay. When I turned back around, I caught a glimpse of something flashing in the sun and, when I saw what it was, I almost couldn't believe it.

There, standing in a grassy area about 20 yards from the field I was mowing, was the trophy I'd always dreamed of—and then some. The rack on this buck was phenomenal. I'd hunted most of my life, and I'd taken more than 50 deer in that time. But I've never wanted anything as much as I wanted that buck.

A month later, I caught a glimpse of the buck while bowhunting, but the opportunity for a shot never presented itself. The next time our paths crossed—the last day of November, 1998—things would be different. It was opening day of Ohio's gun deer season. The wind was out of the west and quite strong, so stalking the buck near what I thought was his bedding area seemed like the best option. Moving ever so slowly, I crept up to the spot where I expected to claim my prize. Instead, I jumped a 10-pointer. Most hunters would have been elated, but I have to say that I was rather disappointed. I aimed my .44 Magnum at the deer, but I opted not to shoot—in case the big buck was in the area.

After a few more steps, I froze. While peering over the tall grass, I held my breath as I spotted the buck of my dreams nearly 100 yards in front of me. The standoff had officially begun. He was looking toward me. I watched him for at least five minutes before the deer looked away again.

I slowly sank to the ground with a willow against my back and reached for my binoculars. Scanning the area, my fear was confirmed; the deer was gone. Patience was all I had left at that point, so I waited. Nearly a half-hour had passed when I realized his eyes were fixed on me. At first I thought his monstrous rack was part of the trees . . . until I saw his head when he looked the other way. I did not move, although time was of the essence. I had less than 30 minutes to figure out what to do.

Realizing I had to move in on him, I crept forward with the wind still in my favor. After gaining 20 yards, I decided not to push my luck for fear of spooking him. The deer moved south, in and out of the cover, and suddenly stopped in a clearing. That was my chance. The perfect opportunity was presenting itself about 70 yards in front of me.

With the barrel of my scoped handgun resting on my knee and the animal in my crosshairs, I squeezed off the shot. The hollowpoint's "pop" was all I needed to assure me that I'd hit my target.

The great buck ran, but I did not follow. Tracking him would have only kept him moving on adrenaline, and my chances of finding him would have been diminished. Instead, I

OHIO BUCK RAISES THE BAR FOR HANDGUNNERS

The buck measured 203 2/8 BTR inches (irregular).

slipped out of the field in hopes he would be dead by the time I returned.

Eating was really the last thing I had on my mind, but a quick dinner would at least kill some time. Much less anxious than I had been an hour earlier, I returned to the place where I hoped to stake my claim. Still, I began to get a little nervous. It was 6:30 at night. The wind was so gusty, I didn't expect to find any hair near the area where I shot.

After 15 minutes of circling the area, I found his tracks but no blood. I decided to return to the last place I saw the animal. I started circling again. After only five minutes, I gasped as I saw a huge rack in the tall grass. My heart pounded faster the closer I got to the buck—the most awesome I had ever seen. He would score 203⅜.

12

Sportswoman's Paradise

Hunter: Carol Fairbanks
BTR Score: 175 5/8
Date Taken: Nov. 8, 1999
Irregular; Compound Bow

I held high hopes for Louisiana's 1999–2000 hunting season. I waited all summer and fall, counting the days until I could take my brand new bow to the woods and arrow my first deer with it. My boss' surveillance cameras had photographed some wonderful bucks, and we had invested a lot of time scouting. As opening day drew near, I felt I was ready. I also thought that I knew right where to find the deer.

While this was Carol Fairbanks's first deer with a compound bow, she was well prepared when the 15-pointer crossed her path in Louisiana.

    The night before the opener, I tossed and turned in my bed, trying to sleep. I had spent two weeks preparing for the morning to come: washing hunting clothes, assembling my equipment, practicing with my bow, fletching arrows and anything else that I could possibly think of that might give me an edge. I finally found sleep around 2:30 a.m.

    Two hours later, my alarm was beeping. I felt like I had just gone to sleep, mostly because I had. So much for an edge!

I hunted long hours that weekend with high hopes. But there was not much excitement and lots of disappointment. I did not see any bucks, and even does and yearlings were sparse.

Still, I spent a lot of time in the woods, ever hopeful, thanks to my non-bowhunting husband's willingness to baby-sit our children during the ensuing weeks. But my disappointment continued. Where had the deer gone? Before hunting season, there were lots of deer. Now I wasn't seeing any!

I was just about to give up when I decided to move to a different part of the woods. After scouting a little more, I found the perfect place for a stand in a section of woods where no other stands existed—overlooking a brand new road that had been cut at the beginning of the season.

I put up my stand on Wednesday, Nov. 3, where the road came to a "T." Heavy cover was everywhere except for the road, and there was a deer trail crossing both roads, leading into a ravine and emerging in a soybean field that had just been harvested. The palmettos were 8 feet tall, and thick briars were everywhere else.

I went back to that stand the following Monday afternoon—later than I wanted—and was in place shortly after 4:00. Despite the presence of a few mosquitoes, conditions were wonderful. There was little or no wind, and the sun was setting at my back. Everything was quiet and still.

Once situated, I pulled out my paperback and settled in for the hunt. I had only been reading about 20 minutes when the palmettos started to snap, crackle, and pop. Since I could no longer concentrate on my book, I rolled it up and put it in my shirt pocket. The palmettos were moving all around me, and the time started to fly.

"All these deer are so close to me," I thought as palmettos within 25 yards began wiggling. "It's going to get dark without me seeing a one."

I was wrong.

At about 5 p.m., I heard a deer step into my road just out of sight. Through the brush, I could barely glimpse parts of deer bodies and feet walking on the road toward me. My anxiety grew as I waited for the deer to step around the curve and into view. With bow in hand, ready to draw, my heart relaxed when a doe and her two yearlings stepped around the bend.

As I watched the three deer feed down the road in front of me, I tried to stop my knees from jerking. The deer had been feeding under me for about 10 minutes when I heard the palmettos starting to rattle again. Not letting myself get too excited this time, I waited. It was about 5:10 p.m. and almost dark.

Again, I heard several deer step into the road about where the others had exited the tangle of palmettos. I waited for the new arrivals to walk into view as the light continued fading. Would I have time?

The lead deer was a monstrous buck. When he stepped around the curve, he was facing me. I immediately knew that he was a trophy of a lifetime.

My bow was in hand and I was ready to draw, but he was looking directly at me. I was about to panic, thinking, "This deer is going to walk right on out of sight without me even getting a shot."

But I knew from experience that I would rather not get a shot, and keep him unaware of my presence, than make a wrong move and spook the buck.

The more I thought about it, the more nervous I became, especially since I had never harvested an animal with my bow. That's when I started paying attention to the deer behind the monster. There was a 16- or 17-inch typical 8-pointer next in line. Behind him was another bruiser buck. I could only see parts of the third buck, but I knew he was large. I was seeing his antlers over the brush, and that alone was spectacular.

Through all the excitement, I hadn't realized that when the bucks came up, they had scared the doe into the palmettos. Her newly abandoned yearlings stood between the lead buck and me. As I wondered how I was going to get off my shot, the doe emerged from the palmettos to retrieve her youngsters. The buck turned and looked back at the commotion.

Finally, at 5:20 p.m., I drew my bow and released the arrow in one motion. I saw my fletching bury into the buck, and he crashed off through the palmettos. Although I knew that a hit doesn't necessarily mean a deer on the ground, there was no stopping my adrenaline. After a lot of effort, I found my way to the ground and eased over to where he'd stood.

Not yet composed enough to trail the deer myself, I began calling for help. My boss, John Mark Stutson, was just through the woods about 200 yards on a stand. He heard me and headed my way. I took off in his direction, and we met halfway. When he saw me, I was jumping up and down and could only babble.

After a short wait, we began tracking my buck in the dark. The trail was easy to follow. He'd only traveled about 45 yards.

It was unbelievable! He was just as big as I remembered—a massive 15-pointer. My boss was almost as thrilled as I was. The 5½-year-old buck registered 175⅝ inches as an irregular on the BTR scale, soaring into the record book with more than 70 inches to spare.

Over the next few weeks, I stayed busy taking him all over Louisiana, entering him in big buck contests and telling the story. Despite all the hoopla, I couldn't help thinking about that other buck. He was still out there somewhere, and I was pretty sure that he would stay in the area since he had no idea what had happened to his buddy.

SECOND VERSE

When gun season opened, I took my rifle back to the same area. I was gunning for the other buck!

Day after day, week after week, I went back to the same area. After nearly giving up the chase, the 18-inch wide 12-pointer finally stepped into my road with his head down on Jan. 14. I was ready!

At the shot, the deer crashed off through the underbrush. I thought that I'd hit him hard, but there were no signs (I had shot the buck in the neck, above the shoulder). Going for my boss, once more, I was a mess. I was totally convinced that I would never find the buck. For a moment, I even wished that I had missed.

In leaving, however, the deer left broken palmettos and briars in his wake. My boss and I followed the path right to him not 50 yards from the road. Had I been shooting my bow, he would have made "Buckmasters Whitetail Trophy Records," too. But the rack, while impressive, fell just shy of the 140-inch firearms minimum.

13

It Pays to Have Friends

Hunter: Rodney Osowski
BTR Score: 161⅝
Date Taken: Oct. 2, 1998
Typical; Compound Bow

As so often happens, even for experienced hunters like Rodney Osowski (who has 10 trophy bucks in the Buckmasters record book, all taken with a compound bow in his home state of Minnesota), the news about a buck with a huge set of antlers came from a friend, his brother's employer, who happened to see it cross a highway to feed in a soybean field during the harvest week.

As Rodney had permission to hunt the property next to where the buck was spotted, he immediately checked out the

This fine buck, which fell to Rodney Osowski's arrow, scored 161⅞ (typical) in the BTR scoring system.

area. It was an overgrown pasture that had not been in use for many years. Burr oak and popple (aspen) were starting to creep back in, along with some basswood trees. He found a good place to hang a stand between a small creek and a manmade dugout that had been used to build a dike around the landowner's yard. Rodney knew that if the big buck came his way, it would likely be on the deer trail that ran down this natural funnel. Rubs in the area also indicated that a big buck was present.

It was well before the rut on a sunny, mild day in early October when Rodney had a chance to slip out after work and get to his stand about 12 miles away. He had been waiting for the right wind to hunt, and after a couple of days of putting off the hunt he finally had it. The southwest wind had changed to a northwest wind, which was ideal as the stand was placed back from the trail facing east.

At around 5:45, after an hour or so in the stand, a young 8-point buck came into view and continued on the trail until he

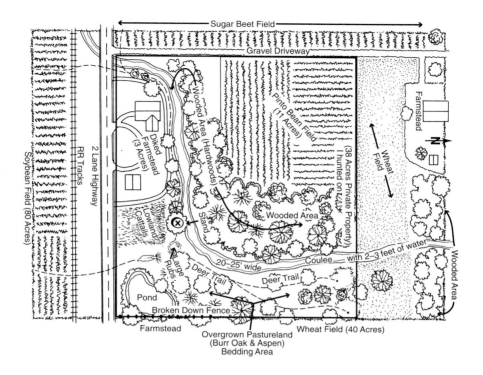

was right below Rodney's stand. He stopped to sniff the tree steps Rodney had attached to the tree trunk to help him reach the stand. Evidently, he smelled a trace of the doe urine still on the rubber gloves that Rodney had used to place the attractor scent around the stand and left on when he climbed up.

As Rodney continued to keep a cautious eye on the buck below him, he saw the deer's head snap around to the east. Sure enough, another buck was milling around and slowly making its way down the trail. Due to the cover, Rodney couldn't clearly see the rack until the buck had moved to within 25 yards or so. What he saw almost made him fall out of his stand. It was definitely the buck he'd heard about, and it was carrying the largest rack he figured he'd ever get a shot at with a bow. At 15 yards he

Brothers Rodney and Randy Osowski have accounted for an amazing total of 13 records in "Buckmasters Whitetail Trophy Records."

had a full frontal shot, but with the experience of many years afield, chose not to take it.

The buck turned down to the creek and took a drink, and Rodney used this chance to get ready for a shot—slowly, of course, because he still had to be careful not to spook the young 8-pointer directly beneath the stand. Finally, the younger buck moved past the tree about 15 yards while the big buck remained standing near the creek, giving Rodney a little breathing room. After what seemed like an eternity, Rodney saw the buck moving back up from the creek. He had a clear shot quartering away at 15 yards and quickly released his arrow. He knew it was a good hit, but the arrow did not pass through. He watched the buck run for about 60 yards until he was out of sight, hoping to hear the sound of the buck crashing in a heap, but no sound came to him.

Night was coming on, and after waiting three hours he was back with a lantern to follow up the blood trail. He was able to track the buck for 70 yards or so and found three spots where the deer had bedded down before moving on. Then there was no more blood to follow, and he had no choice but to leave the buck overnight. Even though he hadn't jumped the buck yet, he had to be very careful not to push him too hard because he was only a quarter-mile from posted land.

The following morning Rodney returned with his uncle to take another run at the blood trail. They found the lantern hanging where he'd left it to mark the end of the trail the night before and began to look around. An extensive search on the east side of the creek as far up as the posted land turned up nothing. After hours of searching they kicked up a deer with large hoof prints on the west side of the creek and decided to head in that direction. As a last resort, Rodney made a small drive on that side of the creek to see if he could push the buck toward his uncle. About 80 yards into the drive he found the buck dead with the arrow still in him. The arrow had entered behind the shoulder of one side and buried itself in the opposite shoulder. The Muzzy broadhead had done its job, and the big buck was down right across the creek from where Rodney had left the lantern the night before.

He had 13 scoreable points with a 19⅞-inch inside spread, totaling 161⅝ BTR points, and Rodney had yet another record-book buck to his credit.

14
Family Affair

**Hunter: Randy Osowski
BTR Score: 157 2/8
Date Taken: Nov. 10, 1991
Semi-Irregular; Shotgun**

Like his brother Rodney, Randy Osowski has several trophies in the "Buckmasters Whitetail Trophy Records." One of his favorite hunts was back in the early 1990s when he and Rodney were hunting the rut in mid-November in Marshall County, Minnesota.

It was late afternoon on a Saturday, and Rodney had just taken a large doe that they were beginning to field dress. They happened to glance into the field to the west of the land they had been

Randy's best buck, taken with a shotgun, scored a total of 157 2/8 (semi-irregular) BTR.

hunting and saw several deer—and a particularly large buck—running around. As the rut was on, the buck was keeping quite busy. The land the deer were on was posted and all they could do was watch, but the brothers knew from numerous scouting trips and previous hunts that there were several well-traveled deer trails from that field into the 40-acre woodlot where they did have permission to hunt. Visible scrapes and rubs in the area also indicated that at least one veteran buck had been using the woodlot.

    Rodney suggested that they set up ground blinds along the primary trail through the woodlot the following day, just in case the big buck decided to come their way. The woods they were using consisted mostly of mature oak, elm, and ash trees, and the area was bound by a river on the north side and by cultivated farm fields to the east, south, and west.

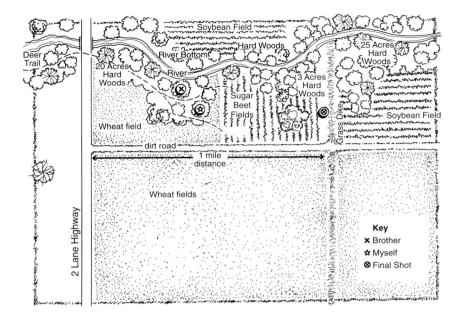

With the wind out of the north the next morning, they set up their blinds on the south side of the deer trail most likely to be used and around 30 yards back from it—plenty close enough for Randy to be in easy shotgun range if the big buck ambled down the trail. It was a simple matter to arrange makeshift blinds from downed timber in the woods. Randy and his brother had applied Wildlife Research Scent Killer to control any human odor and placed some Tink's #69 along the trail in several spots to attract, and hopefully hold, the big buck's attention in a clear shooting lane.

It was a cold, clear morning, around 25 degrees with snow on the ground, when the brothers made plans to meet at noon for lunch and then settled into their blinds to see what would be moving that morning. It wasn't long before they heard shooting to the west of their position, and they figured that another hunting party, located around a mile and a half in that direction, had targeted the buck they'd seen the previous day. There was nothing to do but wait and see.

Apparently no one had gotten the buck, because a little while later he came trotting right down the trail the brothers had hoped he'd use. He was following several does, incautious and in broad daylight—as the rut will make even smart, old bucks drop their guard. The deer were not running, but not walking, either.

As he was using an open sight on his shotgun, Randy decided to put the whole bead on the buck. As it passed broadside at around 30 to 35 yards, he calmed himself and pulled the trigger. The deer buckled then steadied and took off at a full run for another patch of woods to the east of their location. A few minutes later, Rodney appeared to see if Randy had taken the buck they'd been keying in on. Randy knew the buck had taken a solid hit, but he was afraid it was a little too far back for a quick-killing shot. As it was already 11:30, they decided to have lunch and give the buck time to lie down and relax.

They waited around an hour and half before starting to trail the buck. There were specks of blood along the trail and they could see where he had entered the next patch of woods. Rodney volunteered to go around to the other side of the woodlot and try to push the buck back toward his brother. As Rodney began his one-man drive through the woods, Randy saw several deer slide out, but not his buck. He waited tensely as he caught glimpses of his brother occasionally through the woods. He could hear him moving noisily along, but still no buck. Finally, towards the last 20 to 30 yards of the woods, Rodney kicked up the buck and he barreled out right in front of Randy. This time when he shot, the buck stayed down.

He field dressed at 210 pounds and scored 157⅝, with 16 scoreable points and a 25-inch spread.

15

Bruiser from Bull Creek

*By Jim Ward
(as told by Charles McLaughlin)*

**Hunter: Charles McLaughlin
BTR Score: 227 4/8
Date Taken: Nov. 25, 1997
Irregular; Rifle**

In the summer of 1997, I spotted a big buck that kept my heart rate elevated until Nov. 24, opening day of West Virginia's gun deer season. That day couldn't arrive fast enough. I was ready before I even climbed between the sheets the night before, and I rose early. The moon was still shining as I pulled out of my driveway.

Charles McLaughlin with the West Virginia buck that put him in the record book. The buck scored 227 4/8 (irregular).

Hunting season is very big in southern West Virginia. All the local restaurants open early for the hunters. After a big breakfast and three cups of coffee, I wished everyone good luck and headed for Bull Creek, a five- or six-mile drive. I was excited; had been for more than a week. I had been counting the days.

Bull Creek is a hollow about four or five miles long. There are very few houses, and it's a good place to hunt. The mountains are very high and beautiful there. I drove my Volkswagen to the head of the hollow, found a place to park and started up the hollow by flashlight. It was still dark when I reached the top.

"So far, so good," I thought. Now all I have to do is wait for him to show. With a little mountain luck, I'd get the trophy buck I had dreamed about that night. I chose a spot at the base of a big pine tree just below the ridge where he and several does had been running. I cleaned out a spot where I could move noiselessly, turned off my light, and sat in the darkness. I heard only the distant hooting of an owl.

These West Virginia deer usually move down the mountain at night. Just before daybreak, they start their journey back toward their high-country beds. When dawn broke, however, I saw nothing. As the sun climbed higher, I watched squirrels carry nuts to their winter homes. After a few hours of it, I convinced myself that nothing was going to happen. I lit a cigar and headed home.

The next day began in much the same way. After a big breakfast at the restaurant, I wished all the other hunters good luck and headed for the big pine tree on top of the mountain.

I quietly slipped up the mountain and took my position against the same tree. Downhill from me was a pine thicket. I heard a noise in there and turned to see a deer. I did not know whether it was a doe or a buck until it moved into a small clearing. Then I recognized it—the big buck for which I had been waiting. Two does and a couple of smaller bucks were with him. I kept waiting for a chance to shoot, but it didn't come until he moved into a small opening between the pines. Just as I was preparing to squeeze off a shot, they spooked.

I shot three times as the big buck jumped, but I hit nothing but the wind. I was totally discouraged. The chance I had waited on for so long had just disappeared along with the deer. My hopes for getting the big one were gone! I sat beneath the tree for a while, chomping a cigar, before I decided to call it quits and started down the mountain. I heard a noise just before two does almost ran over me. It was too late to get the big one, I thought, but maybe I could get one for the freezer.

I went back to my seat beneath the big pine tree and waited.

I had been sitting there only a few minutes when I heard something behind me. I looked around the tree to see a big buck coming straight downhill toward me at a dead run. He was not as big as the one I'd missed, but he was a nice deer. Just as he crossed over the hill toward the pine thicket, I shouldered my gun and started to shoot. Before I could squeeze the trigger, however, I saw the biggest set of antlers I had ever seen in my life, coming over the hill behind the first buck. The big buck was chasing the smaller one down the hill.

Since he was running, I couldn't do anything but whistle and try to stop him. The first two times, he never heard me. On my third attempt, he slowed to a walk, still heading for the small pines. I knew that if he got to the thicket, I'd have no shot. When he turned downhill, the big pine tree hid me long enough to get the gun to my shoulder without being seen. When he turned again, at 75 yards, he stepped into my crosshairs. I fired two shots, both hitting home. Either would have taken him.

Although I knew he was big, I had no idea his rack was as huge as it was. He had antlers coming off antlers. I quit counting points when I got to 20—missing another 10. I lit a cigar, sat there awhile, and admired him, hardly believing what I had just done. After I field-dressed him, I hid him under some brush and went for help in getting him off the mountain. No one had ever seen anything like it! I pulled over many times on my way home to show him to other hunters who had motioned me to stop.

The buck scored 227⅝.

16

Pee Dee Buck is No Pee Wee

Hunter: Hunter Norman
BTR Score: 166 2/8
Date Taken: Oct. 23, 1998
Irregular; Blackpowder Rifle

On Oct. 22, 1998, my friend, Rick Anderson, and I loaded up our deer stands and headed to the Pee Dee Wildlife Refuge in Anson County, North Carolina. We walked far away from the roads, searching for a couple of good and secluded spots to hunt during the next two days. We found ourselves walking some of the hardwood ridges while scouting for some promising sign.

Hunter Norman with the monster he took from the Pee Dee Wildlife Refuge in Anson County, North Carolina.

I had bowhunted the general area two years earlier—the only time I had done any serious scouting before that day. But I felt confident that we had chosen a good area because I had also spent some time going over topo maps with the Anson County farm extension agent. My only worry was that the maps were a few years out of date.

We saw plenty of sign as we moved toward the area I had in mind, but the type of sign I was seeing was not the kind I had hoped to find. I did not see any big rubs or scrapes that looked like they belonged to a big mature buck. Most of the stuff I was seeing appeared to have been made by smaller ones. I was a little discouraged. Our only advantage was that we had put a lot of distance between the nearest access road and us.

We saw six does and a buck ahead of us in a thicket when we got to within 200 yards of where we were intending to hunt.

Since we had not found the sign we had hoped for, we decided to put one stand up to see into the thicket. While Rick put up his stand, I walked about 400 yards farther to a spot that had looked promising on the topo map. I found the general area about 30 minutes before it started getting dark, so I quickly picked a tree and put my stand on its trunk. After mine was hung, we made a quick exit, trying to minimize our scent and allow the woods to settle. That night, I told Rick that I did not think we were in the best place, but we would make due.

The temperature had dropped into the 30s the next morning. This was the first good cold snap of the year, and it made us feel more confident that the deer would be active. We arrived at the parking area around 5:15 a.m. because we wanted to be in our stands well before daylight. Since it was a long walk, I did not wear my coat. Instead, I put it in my backpack so that I would not start sweating.

After the trek to my stand, I climbed the tree and settled in my perch. Thirty minutes later, I could hear deer walking in the woods in front of me. A few deer walked within a couple of yards of the bottom of my tree, crossed my entry path, and kept going right past me—heading toward Rick.

As it finally got light enough to see around 7:15, I saw a deer moving to my left. My first impression was that the deer was a buck because of the shape of his neck. As I watched the deer through my binoculars, I could tell that it was an 8-pointer with exceptionally white antlers. The deer never would turn his head fully toward or away from me, so I could not tell how wide he was.

From what I could see (a side view) the tine length was not that great. He slowly wandered behind some thicker brush, and I could not see him anymore. Twenty or 30 minutes later, I saw five or six deer moving through the woods where I had seen the buck earlier. They were all does as far as I could tell. They started feeding on acorns under the white oaks that were on the ridge to my left. The ridge angled in front of me about 40 yards away, so I hoped they would feed in front of me and that they would bring someone else to dinner. That's when I heard a stick break loudly behind me, and I could hear a deer moving through the woods at a quick pace. Because the deer was moving quickly, I stood up and tried to locate the animal before he got right on top of me.

The deer stopped just a few yards short of a small clearing about 20 yards distant. I finally saw him through my binoculars. He was looking up the ridge before he stepped into the open. The deer grunted a couple of times and started walking on a path that would take him nearly under my tree.

The buck was one of the biggest cowhorns I have seen in the last couple of years. His beams were about 15 or 16 inches long. The deer walked within five yards of my tree and went up on the ridge in front of me and out of sight without stopping again. He evidently knew where he wanted to go.

Having seen seven or eight deer in the past hour, I was on full alert by 8 a.m., scanning the area for deer easing along the hardwood ridges. The woods were alive with noise from squirrels and birds feeding in the tops of the trees, and the sun was just about to break through the trees and bring some welcome warmth. Since I had not yet put on my jacket, I was a bit chilled. I started to put my jacket on, but decided not to because the movement might scare any deer away that I could not see. There had been probably 20 shots in the distance, too—proof that the deer were on the move. None of the shots were very close to us, and I hoped it would stay that way.

As I was scanning the woods, I saw a doe walking in a clear sunny area between the trees. She stopped and looked back over her shoulder and slowly raised her tail. She stood there for a few seconds, then ran a few steps and stopped again. She looked back again before running. I got ready for a quick shot if a good buck was following the doe. I kept watching the area where she had been, feeling that a buck would show himself at any moment. After about 20 minutes, I figured that any deer following the doe must have gotten through when I was scanning other parts of the woods or had passed behind the small opening in the thick undergrowth. The doe had been almost at the absolute limit of how far I could see.

Squirrels were now running all over the forest floor, making it impossible to hear a deer walking in the dry leaves. A squirrel in the tree above me was feeding heavily on white oak acorns and dropped one directly on the aluminum platform of my deer stand. The noise was something that no deer hunter wants to make while hunting. I looked up the tree at the squirrel and had to fight back the temptation to try to scare him to another tree. That was a wise decision. As I began scanning the woods again, I saw him.

The buck was standing about 75 yards to my right with his head obscured by the limbs of a small tree. As I looked at him through my binoculars, I could not see his rack very well because he was raking it through the limbs. When he stopped toying with the tree, I could see his right side. The deer looked like a definite shooter. As soon as my brain told me to put down the binoculars, the deer turned his head and looked away from me. Although the tree mostly hid the deer's rack, I could see that the tips of the P-2s looked about 20 inches apart!

Suddenly the buck swung his head around and looked in my direction. There was no mistake about it: I was looking at a monster with at least a 20-inch spread. I waited for the deer to turn his head before I made a move to get my gun. When he finally looked away, I traded by binoculars for my muzzleloader. He started walking broadside to me as I brought the gun up to my shoulder. I can remember telling myself to aim a little low at that range, because my rifle had been sighted to shoot three inches high at 100 yards.

As I began to squeeze the trigger, the gun went off just as the buck's head began to pass behind some brush. I saw him flinch and kick his back feet in the air before he dashed. He immediately turned around and ran back in the direction from which he had come. From the time I first saw the deer until the shot, 15 seconds could not have passed.

Rick immediately called me on the walkie-talkie to ask if I had shot. Wanting to try to hear the deer's retreat, I meant to turn the volume down on the radio. Instead, I had turned it wide open. When Rick called again, it nearly made me jump out of the tree. I grabbed the radio and told Rick that I had shot a really nice deer. His response was, "How big?"

All I could tell him was that he was about 20 inches wide, had a lot of mass on his P-2s, and I felt that the shot had been good. I decided to wait about 30 minutes before trying to trail the buck. After about 10 minutes, however, I could not stand the suspense and got down and slowly walked to the spot. With other hunters in the woods, I did not want him to go far if he was wounded.

I could not locate any blood, although I did see where he had kicked up the leaves at the shot. I could easily follow his tracks to where he had turned and slid in the leaves. As I started looking ahead where I lost sight of him, I saw the buck lying on the ground about 15 yards in front of me. I was overjoyed. From the odd way that he was lying on the ground, however, I thought that he was going to jump up and run off because his head was upright and he appeared to be hiding from me.

As I approached the deer slowly, ready for a follow-up shot, it became clear why his head was in an upright position. When the deer went down, his head came to rest about six inches off the ground on top of a limb that had fallen out of a tree. Also keeping his head level was an eight-inch drop tine!

The deer was massive, tipping the scales at 223 pounds. He had seven points on his right beam and 12 on his left. I called Rick and told him that he would not believe the deer I had shot and to get down and come see it. I was so excited that I could hardly speak slowly enough to be understood. I have been fortunate to take my share of very nice bucks, but this one beat all I had ever dreamed of seeing.

17

Trapper John's Buck

**Hunter: John Schmidt
BTR Score: 171 7/8
Date Taken: Nov. 3, 1994
Semi-Irregular; Compound Bow**

John Schmidt hunts and traps in the state of Louisiana, and that means working in hot weather. Trapping a variety of animals and spending time afield in all seasons has given "Trapper John" an uncanny feel for the woods near his home.

He'd been hunting for several weeks in an area he was very familiar with one autumn when he returned to his stand early in the afternoon on an 80-degree November day, seeking a particularly large buck rumored to be in the vicinity. Piecing to-

TRAPPER JOHN'S BUCK

Trapper John Schmidt with his 171⅞-point buck and two other Louisiana trophies. *(photo by Luke Ducote)*

gether reports from several acquaintances, John had been able to pinpoint the area where the buck made regular appearances and secure permission to hunt there. A good deal of scouting had shown him a series of rubs that could only be from a sizeable buck. As Louisiana is not known for producing a lot of bucks this size, John was keen to be the first to have a shot at him.

The rut had not yet begun, and John was hunting from a treestand of his own making that overlooked a good area of transition cover that deer funneled through on their way back and forth between feeding and bedding areas. The rub line on a group of cedar trees was within view of the stand, and John felt confident he'd have a chance at the buck he wanted.

Years of experience with treestands had left him less than satisfied that they wouldn't make a telltale noise at an inopportune moment, and John had decided to build his own stands from expansion metal and EMT, stands he could guarantee would be 100 percent silent when he needed them to be.

He had also learned to be extremely careful to control his own scent when hunting in such hot, muggy weather. He followed a program of washing his hunting clothes in Sport Wash and then hanging them outside for a week or so before packing them in layers of dried green pine needles in a black plastic bag between seasons. He also used rubber boots and scent-control clothing as an extra edge.

He got to his stand early that afternoon for the evening hunt, around 2:00, making sure to keep absolutely quiet. He saw several bucks but decided to pass because he knew that rare big buck was likely to be in the area. Around 4:30 just the buck he was looking for came down the trail from the north, offering him a clear shot straight down from 35 feet. It was a tough shot that would have to hit the spine, but it was also the only chance he was going to get. John steadied himself and let fly. The arrow found its mark, but hit a little to the right of the spine, and John, with his heart in his throat, watched the deer bolt off before climbing down and heading back to the truck to get out of the hot clothing he'd been wearing.

After giving the buck some time to relax, John and a friend came back to track the deer. They found no blood on the ground at first and then just a drop or two high on the brush, but the buck's path through the high weeds was plainly visible, and the tracks he had dug when turning to leap away were also easy to spot. John took the lead, cautiously following the trail until he entered a very thick patch of briars, where he suddenly found himself face to face with the buck, which obviously didn't want to move until it absolutely had to.

Afraid that the buck would bolt right out of the country and with no time to bring his bow up, the instincts John had developed while trapping over 2,800 wild boar took over. He reached out without thinking and caught a hind leg as the deer turned to run, and the huge deer dragged him 50 feet through the brambles, which tore at his body from every angle, but not enough to make him release his hold on the best buck he'd seen in that part of the country. Finally, the wounded deer tired and began to slow down, giving John a chance to regain his composure. He swiftly stepped on the buck's large antlers to anchor its head and knelt on its chest as he put his knife through the heart, just as he'd done with countless boar over the years.

On closer examination, he saw that the arrow had penetrated one lung and also damaged the buck's liver.

They put the deer on a scale whole and it registered a whopping 326 pounds, with a rack that scored 171⅞ in the BTR scoring system.

18

On a String: The BTR's No. 1 Typical by Recurve

By Richard W. Peterson

Hunter: Mike Burroughs
BTR Score: 154 4/8
Date Taken: Nov. 19, 1999
Typical; Recurve Bow

Moments after Mike Burroughs started tickling his rattling horns together, he spotted a buck at 100 yards. It was following the scent trail that he'd laid prior to climbing into his treestand.

ON A STRING: THE BTR'S NO. 1 TYPICAL BY RECURVE

Mike Burroughs took this trophy in southeastern Iowa with a recurve bow. It scored 154⅜ (typical) in the BTR system. *(photo by Richard W. Peterson)*

"He came in on a string, taking the trail I had set up for him," said the Iowa bowhunter. There was no need to continue rattling or to puff on a grunt call as long as the animal was coming his way, so Mike merely had to keep his cool as his heart thundered in his chest.

Mike had spotted the buck a few days earlier as it was bedded with a doe. He'd chosen to hunt that particular spot in the hope that the big deer would not stray too far. His stand overlooked one of three trails entering the woodlot from an open field.

Based on what he observed in the off-season that year (1999), Mike had a good idea of where to hunt and when. His scouting is not limited to a few pre-season excursions. He keeps at it the year-round, even if he has other reasons for being in the woods.

"I start going to the timbers in February, hunting for (shed) antlers," he said. "And I continue going until the mushroom season ends in May. Then I spend the summer months visiting the areas where the bigger ones might be.

"It also helps to have hunted an area for several years, knowing where the bucks hang out and their tendencies," he continued. "Finding the best spots is kind of like bass fishing. If a few big ones are caught—or shot—in certain spots, there is a chance that others might come in because of the habitat."

He saw the record book buck during one of his visits to a funnel popular with the local whitetails. The woodlot, surrounded by a creek, an old road, and a cut soybean field, also contained some prime bedding habitat. He'd often seen a group of deer in there that included a 150-class buck. It was a great buck, but it was not the monster that finally spurred him into choosing a stand site and clearing a shooting lane.

"I found the trail with the best shooting lanes," he said. "In this case, it was the one I would have to clear the least brush from to get good shots from a treestand. I don't like messing too much with the terrain. I had to remove just a little extra brush."

After he'd cleared the few obstructions, Mike decided to avoid the place for three or four days. He returned on the morning of Nov. 19, when the wind was minimal and blowing in his favor.

Before climbing his tree, as is his custom, Mike doused a drag rag with Mrs. Doe Pee's estrous doe urine and laid down a scent line for about 100 yards. Then he re-juiced the rag and returned to his tree via the same trail, giving it what he calls "double coverage."

When the buck crossed that trail shortly after hearing Mike's rattling, it kept its nose to the ground all the way to within 15 yards. When Mike shot, the deer went down after traveling only 25 yards.

The veteran bowhunter had arrowed a 13-pointer that would later prove to be the largest "typical" ever taken with a recurve bow in "Buckmasters Whitetail Trophy Records."

Burroughs visited this well-worn trail three days earlier and cleared away some small limbs to open up a shooting lane. That visit, a clear head, and the estrous doe urine that he used to doctor the trail get credit for the harvest.

19

Cyclone

Hunter: Robert Nichols
BTR Score: N/A
Date Taken: 2001
Irregular; Compound Bow

It was 1999 when Wallace Nichols, Hunter and Will Meldman, and Christy Nichols first named him. At 4½, he had a small drop tine. Since a hurricane had just passed directly over our lease in Klebers County, Texas, they named him Cyclone. Little did they know how much time and effort we would all spend photographing, analyzing, and finally hunting Cyclone.

Few hunters have the opportunity and skill to keep track of a buck like "Cyclone" for so many years before harvesting it. Robert Nichols (right) has taken half a dozen BTR record-book bucks in Texas with his bow.

Later in 1999 my friend Jason Riggs and I were looking for a management buck or a turkey. Jason was only 10, but already he was a good photographer. On our north fence (shared with Scott Brandon), we found two bucks locked together: Cyclone and Crooked Neck. Crooked Neck was an old buck who had a funny way of cocking his head to make his neck appear crooked. We had already marked him as an "over-the-hill" for someone to shoot. Crooked Neck had gotten the worst of the fight and was so exhausted he could barely stand up. Cyclone, too, was exhausted.

Locked together, they were oblivious to Jason and me. We grabbed our cameras and burned a lot of film. We didn't know how long they had been locked up, but we quickly realized both deer were doomed if we didn't free them. After the photo session, Jason and I set Cyclone free. He was so tired and dazed, he just walked away. Pictures in the cameras were developed and stories told around the campfire.

We couldn't wait to see Cyclone next year at 5½. That winter was wet, and he exceeded our wildest predictions.

By the fall of 2000 Cyclone developed into a 6×6 with double drop tines and several stickers! He was also inconsiderate enough to move across our north fence into Scott Brandon's pasture, becoming his deer. We were convinced he was over 180, but also convinced he was just 5½. What a dilemma. We all decided to let him go another year. We called our neighbor to the east and asked him to save the deer if he saw him. We used a lot more film and video on this magnificent buck, kept plenty of corn near his living room, and kept our fingers crossed we didn't look like fools for showing restraint. Other great deer were killed in 2000, but Cyclone survived. Near the end of the season, he injured his left hip in a fight and developed a limp, but we thought it would go away. Lots of people got a huge pleasure from seeing this great buck.

By the fall of 2001 we couldn't wait to see Cyclone. We spent lots of hours looking, but he was nowhere to be found. Then, in October he appeared in Scott's pasture, just over the fence. We share deer on our common fence and have guidelines about where and how to hunt them. Scott solved any indecision when he called me one day. "Robert," he said, "you saved Cyclone and watched him mature. He's your deer. Go and hunt him in my pasture whenever you want. I'll keep an eye on him but I want you to shoot him." What a gentleman. It helped that Scott has already killed some great deer with his bow, but he made a very generous decision about Cyclone. I'll get even with Scott. I'm not sure how yet, but I will.

CYCLONE

With Scott's permission, Wallace and I began to scout for Cyclone, but he never appeared. We saw him only three times this year, set up in both spots, and he never reappeared. His hip injury still caused him to limp, so we speculated he wouldn't jump the fence or participate in the rut. Then one morning, at 10:00 a.m. he appeared on our side of the fence! A spooky, wild buck. Wallace saw him and told me where to hunt him. It was just 80 steps from the main road in heavy cover. I felt a little foolish, but decided to set up where Wallace suggested. I couldn't wait to get back down from Dallas. I got there on a rainy Friday afternoon, and I didn't see an animal. Saturday morning came wet and windy. No deer, and no Cyclone. One more chance, I said. I was alone at the lease, my whole family had deserted me. I was invited to dinner at the La Sequela by my friend Dan Blanks to meet some other deer hunters. I would have time for a short Saturday afternoon hunt, before driving over. At 5:15 p.m., I hadn't seen a buck. Then right out of his living room, walked Cyclone like he owned the pasture (which I guess he did). He stood facing me forever.

I had the wind. He never saw me, but he was not in a position to shoot. Wait until he turns. Stop shaking. Draw. Wait until he looks away. Stop shaking. Release. Watch the arrow hit. Follow through. After days of chasing Cyclone, it was over just that fast.

I saw and heard the arrow hit. Pride of accomplishment came mixed with sadness over ending the life of a great animal. Would he have lived through the winter with a bad left hip and a limp? I want to think not, but we'll never know.

I waited, then slipped quietly into his living room. He hadn't gone far.

Hunting big deer is all about decisions. The decision to free Cyclone from Crooked Neck. The agonizing decision to pass him at 5½ in a low-fence pasture. We couldn't know 2001 would be a terrible drought. But it was. Cyclone declined in 2001 to a 535, but he still had double drops. Should we have passed again until 7½? Hoped for rain? Hoped for the hip to heal? Hoped he lived and didn't decline? We all talked it out, and decided it was too big a gamble. I think we made the right decision, but then hunting old, big deer is always full of uncertainties.

Robert Nichols has six bow-harvested bucks in the BTR record book.

20

The Bean Field Buck

By Ted Rose

Hunter: Mike Wallace
BTR Score: 199 1/8
Date Taken: Nov. 1, 1993
Irregular; Compound Bow

On Nov. 1, 1993, Mike Wallace was sitting upwind from his deer decoy, feeling the chill of the frosty morning. "As always, I had gotten out of bed in time to arrive at my treestand before daylight," said the fireman from Pendleton, Indiana.

Indiana's archery season had been mostly uneventful to that point. Mike had only seen one 10-point buck, but the deer never came within bow range. But Mike had regularly come

Mike Wallace bagged this massive buck with a compound bow. It tallied 199 1/8 (irregular) in the BTR scoring system.

across some really huge tracks that he thought were made by an even larger buck, perhaps at night. That's the one he really wanted.

November's first morning was somewhat routine. Mike had set out his decoy and sprayed doe-in-heat lure on the mannequin's backside. He had no idea he would soon find himself within spitting distance of the buck he'd dreamed about finding in his sights. And he had no idea the brute would be carrying nearly 200 inches of antler.

A LITTLE BACKGROUND

When scouting and putting up his treestand, Mike said he came across a farmer near where he hunts who said that he had seen a big buck running across a soybean field earlier in the fall.

The news, along with the huge tracks at the edge of the woods, convinced Mike that it was going to be a good year.

After hunting from one of his ground blinds and a treestand without any luck, Mike said he decided to put up a couple of new stands—one overlooking a harvested bean field, the other inside a brushy wooded area. The latter was a perfect funnel through which deer traveled to enter or exit thick cover. And because of the crop rotation that year, the funnel would be a convenient route for deer to take to a food supply.

He didn't know when the deer would come through the area, but they inevitably would. He just hoped that he would be there waiting.

The first few outings were unsuccessful. Mike said he was beginning to think the neighborhood whitetails were avoiding that corner of the woods because of his human scent. However, seeing nine deer cross the bean field one morning gave him enough encouragement to keep up the vigil.

The following day, Mike watched as a small group of bucks played in the picked bean field. He became even more confident, although he was sure the buck leaving the gargantuan footprints was totally nocturnal.

Three days later, Mike's mother-in-law spotted a huge buck with four does at the edge of the field where his treestand was located . . . "Just the right ingredient to inspire a bowhunter to the point where it wasn't easy to sleep, thinking of the big buck," he said.

THE FATEFUL DAY

Two more days passed before he could visit the stand. About 6:30 a.m., a small 6-pointer appeared at about 75 yards.

Mike blew his grunt call, and the buck looked his way. He grunted again, and the young deer stepped out of the woods.

Just as the buck emerged from the trees, a big German shepherd ran from behind Mike's stand and chased away the deer. The dog then returned to the tree in which the hunter sat and started barking at him. Mike said the temptation to shoot the dog was great, but he decided against it. He said he knew better than to harm the dog, since it could be the much-loved pet of a nearby resident.

When the shepherd finally left, Mike said he considered the morning a total failure. Yet he chose to remain patient and to just sit still, hoping something good would happen. Sure enough, about 30 minutes later, the 6-point buck reappeared.

After grunting a few times, the buck snaked in behind Mike's stand and milled around for a few minutes before wandering out of range. It wasn't long before Mike began noticing other deer, too, all moving within the small patch of woods to his left.

He was watching the deer in the distance so intently, he almost didn't notice the doe and fawn which had moved silently to where the 6-pointer had been standing earlier. The doe kept looking over her shoulder as if something was bothering her. All of a sudden, a large bush in the distance began dancing wildly back and forth. The commotion made the hair on the back of Mike's neck stand erect.

At that point, Mike nocked an arrow, snapped on his release, and got into position to shoot. As he was waiting—all of his attention diverted to the bush—there was a snapping sound. Thinking it might be a squirrel, Mike slowly turned to get a better look. Instead, coming toward him at a fast pace was the biggest buck he'd ever seen in the woods. The deer had his nose glued to the scent Mike had put on the trail near the corner of the woods.

With no time to stand up and shoot, Mike drew back his bow and let fly the 27-inch Easton. The big buck showed no sign of being hit. "He simply turned and walked deeper into the woods," he said.

Fearing he had a "bad hit," Mike remained in his stand for another 30 minutes, trying to collect his thoughts and settle his nerves. Then he got down and went to check for blood where he'd last seen the big buck.

About the time he arrived at the place where the buck had been standing, he heard a loud snort. That's when he turned and walked out of the woods, deciding to go get some help to do the trailing. He also wanted to allow more time for the big buck to expire.

He returned with his father-in-law, John Stephenson, three hours later to begin the search. Since Mike is color-blind and the leaves were wet, it was a good idea to have some help trailing the deer. He was relieved to find a good blood trail just a short distance from where he had hit the buck.

After slowly tracking the blood a little farther than 100 yards, the duo found the whitetail lying in a clump of tall grass, antlers pointing skyward.

The right main beam of those antlers was $29\frac{1}{8}$ inches long; $28\frac{5}{8}$ inches on the left. The greatest spread was 24 inches; best circumferences $5\frac{5}{8}$ inches; and the longest tine measured $10\frac{4}{8}$. The rack had 11 scorable points on the right antler and 13 on the left, making it a 24-pointer. Its final BTR (compound bow) score was $199\frac{1}{8}$ irregular.

21
A Sandhills Stalk

Hunter: Randy Turechek
BTR Score: 144 5/8
Date Taken: Dec. 8, 1998
Typical; Blackpowder Rifle

Unlike most whitetail hunters across North America who rely on ground blinds and treestands, Randy Turechek prefers to take his chances on the ground, spotting and stalking. It's a technique more frequently used in the open country of the West on antelope and mule deer, and it's a very difficult way to hunt whitetails. But it seems to suit Randy well. His method has also proven to be quite effective, landing him five impressive Midwestern bucks in the "Buckmasters Whitetail Trophy Records."

A SANDHILLS STALK

Blackpowder hunter Randy Turechek with a 144⅞-inch buck taken in Nebraska.

 He's usually in the field before dawn and hunting hard until dark with his muzzleloader, a Kahnke 94 he swears by, always in hand. When you are walking that much, quality Goretex clothing and boots are vital. Randy also keeps his Stoney Point Monopod close at hand while hunting to steady his shots. He has a variety of other gear, but most of his time is focused on getting into good deer country and moving quietly and using the wind to sight bucks and then sneak within muzzleloader range. Most of the gadgets he owns never make it out of his pack. As with all hunters who consistently take trophy animals, Randy has also developed the patience and discipline it takes to pass on

Turechek's spot-and-stalk technique for whitetails netted him this 140⅝-point buck in South Dakota last year—one of five bucks he's put in the Buckmasters record books.

many bucks he would ordinarily harvest. To work hard all day to get into position for a shot and then hold off is something most hunters can't or won't do. He also credits his success to knocking on a heck of lot of doors in Kansas, Nebraska, and South Dakota in search of quality whitetail habitat to hunt.

Several years ago Randy was hunting in Garden County, Nebraska during the late muzzleloader season in December. He hadn't had a chance to scout this area before the season, but he knew from years of hunting the land there that it always held some good bucks. There was a steady northwest wind blowing across the rolling sandhills that day, and Randy began to walk, stopping frequently to glass the country in front of him and always mindful of keeping himself downwind of the area he wanted to work.

After several hours, his binoculars, an indispensable item for a spot-and-stalk hunter, settled on a deer feeding in a meadow a half-mile away, and he could tell immediately that it was trophy-caliber buck. Now began his favorite part of the hunt—the stalk. He studied the ground between his location and the deer to make sure he would be able to move unseen and then slowly and quietly made his way to within a hundred yards of the buck, being careful to move up slowly with the wind in his face.

When he felt he was getting close to shooting range at around a hundred yards, Randy extended the monopod to prepare for a shot and slowly moved forward a step or two at a time. Suddenly, he saw antler tips as the buck, completely unaware of his presence, began walking right toward him out of a small depression in the meadow. Without time to even think, he quickly dropped to one knee and steadied the muzzleloader on the monopod.

The buck was looking directly at him at 70 yards. He checked his 0-power scope and the head and shoulders filled the entire screen. It was now or never. He centered the crosshair in the middle of the buck's neck and squeezed the trigger. The buck seemed to move in slow motion as Randy watched it through the clearing smoke. It bounded away and disappeared from view in the depression.

Randy reloaded as fast as he could and walked over to the depression, not sure whether he had connected or not, but knowing that a buck could quickly vanish in the rolling sandhills terrain. All his worries were over, though, when he spotted the buck 15 yards away, down for good with a perfect neck shot.

It scored 144⅝ points in the Buckmasters scoring system.

22

South Carolina Hunter Finds Nugget in Nibblet Country

By Brad Roberts

Hunter: Raymond Gay
BTR Score: 180 5/8
Date Taken: Nov. 13, 1999
Typical; Rifle

I looked across the open ground toward the bordering fence line, and less than 100 yards away stood the largest white-tailed buck that I had ever seen. He was at the end of a cedar

SOUTH CAROLINA HUNTER FINDS NUGGET IN NIBBLET COUNTRY

Raymond and friend Ricky Markt at one of the large rubs made by his trophy buck. The buck would eventually score 180⅝ (typical).

break, with his chest almost touching a barbed wire fence. His enormous neck held up a wide set of heavy antlers that, oddly, looked almost bone white."

That's how Raymond Gay of Graniteville, South Carolina, described his 1997 encounter with a bruiser 10-pointer. He was hunting in Nebraska with a friend, Rick Markt, Rick's brother Kevin, and the Markts' father. The deer's body size was impressive, too; he was probably pushing 250 pounds.

Raymond looked at the deer through his scope, and he was ready to shoot until he realized that the animal was on the wrong side of the property line.

"Several seconds went by as we stared at each other. Then he turned and walked away," Raymond said. "It was the hardest, yet easiest thing I ever did. There was no point in using the grunt call. The buck knew what he'd seen."

Raymond would have a hard time shaking the image of that big whitetail strolling nonchalantly away from him.

"For two years, I found it hard to take my mind off that incredible buck," he said.

The southerner could not make it back to Nebraska during the 1998 deer season, but the monstrous buck was always in his thoughts. From afar, Raymond kept tabs on the buck harvest in the vicinity—via e-mail, telephone calls, and outdoors websites. He wanted to know if anyone bagged the buck of his dreams.

Information about "his" deer finally came from a young Nebraska couple who lived nearby. The woman, Angie, claimed to have seen an exceptionally large buck. She told her doubting husband, who mentioned it to Kevin, and he passed the information along to Raymond.

"I was thrilled that my deer was still alive!" he said. "When the '98 season was gone, I set my sights on 1999."

Raymond prepared extensively for his return trip to the Cornhusker State.

"I practiced shooting, as always," he said. "I am fortunate to live in a state with the longest rifle season in the country. I get to observe and take many deer. Rick helped me draw a map of the place, too. And I studied the wind by watching a weather site on the Internet from that area."

When Rick and Raymond arrived in Nebraska the night before the season opened in 1999, they first visited Rick's parents to learn who else would be hunting and where. The following morning, Rick, Kevin, and Kevin's son, Ryan, drove to the other side of the ranch to hunt. Raymond walked to his area, putting out his homemade, warm scent bags along the way. He also used boot scent pads soaked with urine taken from a South

"A thousand thoughts went through my mind," Raymond said. "He was standing at the fence, and he was on our property for sure this time, only 25 yards away, his muscles bunched to jump. I had seen what big bucks did when they got to that field—run as hard as they can! I had to shoot then and there, and drop him . . . that or risk him going onto the neighbor's property and not finding him, or maybe not even getting permission to look."

Fortunately, the giant fell at the crack of Raymond's rifle, and he did not move again.

"He was bigger than I imagined. Two years of dreaming, nightmares, and a lifetime of trying for such a deer were at an end," he said.

23

The Patient Hunter

Hunter: Charles Paxton
BTR Score: 138 4/8
Date Taken: Nov. 3, 1989
Typical; Compound Bow

Charles Paxton and his wife were in the habit of cruising the country roads near where he had permission to hunt in Parke County, Indiana to look for deer in the evenings before the start of hunting season. After his brother-in-law told him that he'd spotted a big buck in a soybean field across from a place Charles had permission to hunt, they spent a few evenings checking the area out in August. It took several trips to catch a

Charles Paxton took this trophy buck with a compound bow. It scored 138⅛ in the BTR system.

glimpse of him, but there he was, a beautiful buck munching away in the soybeans with a huge rack clearly visible.

They spotted him again in September, and Charles was determined to find a way to take him. He scouted and hunted hard throughout October and November and saw several bucks, but not the magnificent soybean buck he still saw in his dreams. When gun season finally came in that year, Charles gained permission to hunt across the road where he'd seen the buck, but he decided to wait until the late bow season to give it another try, as he wanted very badly to take a trophy buck with his bow.

The buck never appeared again that season, but a large rub and numerous tracks showed that he was still in the area.

Charles continued to scout the area over the next several months, managing to see the buck once and confirming several of his bedding areas. When the next season finally arrived, he decided to use his climber treestand to hunt close to these bedding areas, moving around a lot and trying to keep a low profile so the buck wouldn't feel pressured. Every evening he was sure he'd see the buck, and it kept him hunting every chance he got.

Finally, in late October, after an early snowfall, Charles was walking out of the woods after a morning hunt and decided to look for sign in two small fingers of timber that jutted out into a nearby clover field. As he was making his way along the south fork, the buck he'd been waiting for jumped out of the top of it. He caught a glimpse of the back of his rack as he went up the other side. He looked huge! He quickly decided to shift operations to these two fingers.

On November 3rd, after hunting the south finger near the clover field without seeing the buck all morning, Charles decided to ask the man who lived across the field if he had seen any activity in the area. He had; the previous evening the buck had been chasing a doe right through the clover field, following her into the north finger of timber.

So the next evening Charles set up his climber where the north finger joined up with a larger section of timber behind it; walking in from the south through the big timber instead of going through the field this time. There were fresh rubs on two

Charles poses with his son, Jared, and another of the four bow-harvested bucks he has entered in "Buckmasters Whitetail Trophy Records."

large trees right near where he'd decided to set up, and he had a feeling that the timing was finally right.

He climbed into his stand, pulled his bow up behind him, and then dropped a scent rag with doe-in-heat urine on it. He began to grunt call, working the call about every thirty minutes or so. Finally, as dusk approached, he looked to his right and saw the buck coming right toward him. Trying to calm his nerves, Charles eased his bow into position and put his release around the string. The buck, as crafty bucks so often do, held up in a clump of brush around thirty yards to the right of the stand.

It was almost more than Charles could take after a year of hard work on this buck, but he managed to stay patient, even though shooting light was fast disappearing. The buck started to circle in front of the stand and Charles went to full draw as the buck stepped into an opening. He put the 30-yard pin behind the buck's shoulder and released. The buck immediately swung around and bound off in the direction from which he'd come.

As night was closing in, Charles decided his only choice was to wait until the next morning to trail the buck, fearing that trailing him right away might push him too far to recover. He climbed down and left the stand from the same direction he'd come in earlier. After a sleepless night of tossing and turning, Charles and his wife, Sherri, headed back at daybreak the next morning. The first 40 yards of the trail revealed only a couple of spots of blood, and Charles began to worry that it had been a poor hit. But as they moved along the trail toward the front of the timber, they saw the buck lying dead, right where Charles hoped he would be.

The 9-point buck scored 138 4/8 in the Buckmasters scoring system. It wasn't the largest of the four bow-harvested BTR record-book bucks he's taken over the years, but after working that hard on one buck, it felt very good, indeed.

24

The Schoolyard Buck

**Hunter: James L. Newman
BTR Score: 189⅝
Date Taken: Nov. 14, 1996
Irregular; Compound Bow**

After begging the landowner for a decade to allow me to hunt a small corner of his Linn County, Iowa, farm, I finally wore him down with the promise that I'd always hunt alone and only with my bow. I was granted permission to hunt the creek bottom behind an old school.

Six years later, in 1993, I blew a chance at a big irregular there because my ladder stand was too close to the trail he was

James Newman's persistence in gaining access to high-quality whitetail habitat led to his taking this trophy buck with a compound bow.

using. A typical, 150-class 10-pointer beat me the following year—catching me with a grunt call in my hands instead of my bow. In 1995, I saw the irregular buck again, this time from a ground blind, but the doe he was trailing scrambled my plans.

By the time the 1996 season began, my wife knew all about "Mr. Big." So did my buddy, Marvin Larson, who had seen the bruiser while hunting on another farm adjoining the school property. Marvin and I were both hunting him.

I spent a lot of time thinking about how I was going to get this big buck. First, I decided to move my stands. I nixed the idea of putting them too deep into his territory. The obvious choice came when the farm's owner cut multiflora rose bushes in lanes behind the schoolhouse and creek. I couldn't get to that area before the cutting.

The only problem with the stand site was that the wind had to be blowing out of the northeast in order for me to hunt it properly. I am a real stickler when it comes to wind direction and hunting deer, explaining why I have several stands in the woods.

I hunted off and on from late October through the first couple of weeks in November, but rarely saw anything from my new stands. Marvin, however, was looking at whitetails almost every time he went afield. Seeing only three deer in two weeks of hunting was taking its toll on me.

I work in a forge shop and get off at 3 p.m. It was my habit to buzz home and head for the woods, either on foot or via four-wheeler. I found I could be in a treestand in 45 minutes. I was sure that when the rut rolled around and the cornfields were picked, I was going to see that big buck.

One Saturday morning I went to move one of my stands. Then I headed for the ladder on the old school property. As I drove by, good Lord, there he was—that heavy-horned buck I had been after for two years—right under my new stand! I never stopped; kept driving on home. I must have been grinning from ear to ear, too, because my wife said, "Did you see Mr. Big today?" She already knew that I had.

Almost two weeks later, a storm front moved in and the temperature started falling during the day. The wind also began blowing from the northeast. I told my buddies at work I was headed for my new stand. Then the boss said that we were having a meeting after work and that I would have to stay for another half-hour.

That meant that I had to park in sight of my new treestand instead of walking. Still, I grabbed my hunting clothes and

The buck entered "Buckmasters Whitetail Trophy Records" with a score of 189⅝ (irregular).

headed out as quickly as I could. The stand was in a huge maple tree with a perpendicular limb on which I could sit.

I had just climbed up and was taking off my backpack when I saw him between the schoolhouse and me, making his way along the creek. I didn't want to grunt, not yet, because my bow was still hanging on a string. I let him keep walking, telling myself: "Just get yourself belted in, get your bow up, nock an arrow, then grunt all you can."

When I couldn't see him anymore, I decided I didn't have anything to lose by grunting seven or eight times. I looked at my watch. It was 4:30 p.m. I had another 30 minutes or so to hunt—not much time, but enough.

There he was, coming through the rose bushes. "Calm down and do this right," I told myself, "or this old buck will be taking you to school again." He stopped at 40 yards, took a few more steps and stopped again. "Come on, step out into the open. Follow the trail, big guy," I spoke silently.

Instead of following the main trail, he turned and began walking straight toward my tree, following an invisible scent left earlier by a doe. My comfortable seat was going to mess up things, I thought. The limb was pointing right at him. Nevertheless, I drew my bow as he stepped out of the brush and took a bead on the front shoulder.

He turned toward me before I could release. It was 18 yards closer when he turned again, and I let my arrow go—right place, maybe a little ways back. As I watched him leave the area, I knew he was mine. But only if I could find him. The arrow didn't go through him, but all that was hanging out was about six inches of the shaft. He was dragging his right rear leg. He must have been at more of an angle to me than I thought.

I followed the blood trail to a fence about 200 yards away before abandoning the chase. I went for help, calling my bowhunting coach, tracker, friend, and fellow worker, Leon Jones.

"Let's wait and track him early in the morning," he said. "It shouldn't be too hard in the snow." He also kept telling me to be patient, but he wasn't the one who was going to stay awake all night going over that hunt!

We found the 18-pointer the next morning about 200 yards past the fence. His "irregular" rack contained 189⅞ inches of antler by BTR standards.

25

The Swamp Buck

Hunter: Jason Geschke
BTR Score: 126
Date Taken: Oct. 20, 1998
Perfect; Compound Bow

Jason Geschke had been keeping track of a nice buck for a couple of years before he finally had a chance at it. One short deer drive had pushed the deer out of a small swamp two years earlier, although none of the hunters got a shot at him. The following spring, his father had found a large shed antler on a neighboring piece of land where they had permission to scout but not to hunt. He also saw the buck's tracks and caught a few

Jason Geschke with the 126-inch (perfect) "swamp buck" he took with a compound bow.

glimpses of him around the same small cattail swamp that he had been hunting for a few years. In 1998, he finally zeroed in on the buck, and all his hard work and preparation paid off.

The small swamp he was hunting had two small fingers of thick brush and trees, with the north side abutting a road and the south side a field of standing corn. The large tract of woods north of the property (where the large shed antler was found) got hunted pretty hard during the season, and Jason knew that bucks often got pushed into the swampy area he would be hunting.

Jason felt his best advantage was in using the right cover scent for the time of year. In this case, fox scent for a warm evening in October near Racine, Wisconsin.

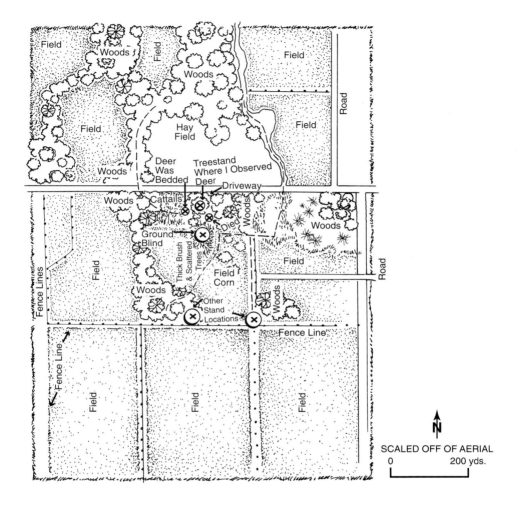

On October 18th, he parked around 80 yards from the swamp and worked his way toward a fence line on the far side of the field where he'd seen two smaller bucks during several scouting trips. But the sight of a large set of tracks crossing in front of where he was parked caught his eye and he stopped to check them out. They showed that a nice buck had headed from the small swamp in the direction of a larger swamp on a neighboring property, so Jason decided to use a stand that overlooked the smaller swamp and gave him a good view of the entire area.

Just before dark, the buck he'd been watching off and on for the last two years walked along a cornrow, down near the end of one of the fingers of timber and brush. He stopped for a moment and then broke into a trot as he headed for the larger swamp, crossing just 40 yards in front of where Jason had parked. The buck had evidently been doing some scouting of his own and knew that Jason usually liked to set up near the back of the property. Ignoring the parked vehicle, he simply made his way to safety using a route that took him away from where he knew danger usually originated. Jason knew he now had the final piece of the puzzle.

After giving it some thought, the following day he set up a makeshift ground blind a few yards back in the finger of timber, giving himself ample room to draw his bow undetected as he looked out over the first few rows of corn. The buck never showed, but Jason was back the next day to try again, confident that he was on the right track.

It was a warm evening and Jason wasn't expecting the buck until close to the end of shooting light. Instead, he appeared two hours early, unusual for October, and coming from a direction opposite of the one Jason had expected. His blind was set back 80 yards from the road, with 60 yards of cattails and another 20 yards of 18-inch-tall grass in the space between. There was just one small tree in the intervening area between hunter and buck, and it was all Jason could do to get his bow up and pointed in the right direction without detection.

The buck made his way through the cattails straight toward the blind. He was almost in full view when he reached the end of the cattails, but the tree still blocked part of his body. Jason had to stay glued to the chair he was using in the ground blind for fear of spooking the buck, but as he was coming from

A fine display of the trophies that Jason has put in the record book.

the left, it still allowed for an easy draw. The buck milled around behind the tree for around 15 minutes and when it finally looked like he might make his way toward the blind on the right of the tree, Jason went to full draw. It was his last chance to do so without being seen and he had no choice but to take it.

The buck's head cleared the tree, but something made him hesitate just nine yards away. Jason was forced to hold at full draw, as he and the buck were almost eye-to-eye with nothing in between. The buck stayed right there, with his head exposed and his vitals still covered by the tree's branches. As Jason struggled to hold his position against fatigue, a car passed on the road and the buck turned to follow the sound. This was all the opportunity Jason needed. He quickly leaned forward in his chair and found a clear shooting lane to just behind the buck's front shoulder, trying desperately to steady an arm that had been holding at full draw for what felt like a good two minutes.

Despite the fact that this movement was completed silently, the buck sensed something amiss and his head spun back to stare directly at the blind. But it was too late, the pin was already centered in the kill zone and Jason released his arrow, sending the broadhead through the deer just behind the shoulder. It bolted through the cattails in the direction of Jason's car but didn't make it 50 yards.

The 5-year-old buck dressed out at 248 pounds with a BTR score of 126, not the biggest of the four bucks he'd placed in the Buckmasters record book with his bow, but certainly the most intense few minutes of hunting he'd ever experienced.

Luckily for Jason, it took the shortest drag of his hunting career to get the buck to his vehicle.

26

Second Chance in Saskatchewan

Hunter: David Pezderic
BTR Score: 206 7/8
Date Taken: Dec. 6, 1996
Irregular; Blackpowder Rifle

I started hunting whitetails again in 1995, after a sabbatical of more than 30 years. My brother in British Columbia, who makes frequent forays into Saskatchewan during hunting season, helped to rekindle that flame. And, like him, I have developed a fanatical interest in learning everything I can about white-tailed deer.

In that sense, I guess you could say the 1997 deer season began for me in 1995. I pored over research material on deer,

David Pezderic's homework allowed him to take this magnificent buck in Saskatchewan.

walked dozens of miles, mapped rub lines and trails, picked up sheds, and became familiar with the habitat. All that paid off in both 1995 and '96, but not like it would in 1997.

Part of my re-schooling included videotaping bachelor groups during the summer. It was on one such trip that a veteran Saskatchewan hunter and I watched a tall and handsome 4×4 in velvet sporting huge eye guards. He could be seen almost each night in his favorite canola field, and he ultimately grew into a fine 4×5, grossing (according to his sheds) somewhere in the 170s.

On opening day of the 1996 muzzleloader season, I scrutinized this deer at 30 yards, eventually passing on him because of the 4×5 frame. The truth is, I did not realize how massive this deer was. I nicknamed him "Curly" because of his long, curving beams. We saw him only rarely after that, except for a few times at dusk.

During the summer of '97, a neighbor spotted a drop-tined buck in the area. I saw it, too. We were convinced it was another deer, not "Curly." We had also filmed another 5×5 a mile or so away with long, sweeping main beams. We thought that one could have been the elusive "Curly."

My brother also watched the drop-tined buck during early bow season. It was in an alfalfa field several hundred yards distant. This sighting proved useful in that it revealed the buck was using a swale in the prairie for concealment as he moved from field to bedding area. From that point on, however, the drop-tined buck vanished. We were still unaware that he was in fact "Curly."

On the morning of Nov. 26, I was cradling my Remington 700 muzzleloader when I finally spotted the drop-tined buck. He was a mile or more away in an opening in the poplar forest and hot on a doe trail. My binoculars revealed the unmistakable drop tine in the pre-dawn light.

Later that day, my 15-year-old son (who was not carrying a firearm) and I set up on a fence line between the aforementioned alfalfa field and a pea field. With bush to the north and south, I knew from the previous two years of scouting that the fence line, in conjunction with the swale in the field, was a favorite travel pattern that would bring the buck to a scrape line on the southern perimeter of the forest.

As we settled in, I told my son that there wouldn't be any action until just about sunset and that there was only a chance in a million that the drop-tined buck would grace us with an appearance. We settled into a relaxed frame of mind in the tall grass, bearing the unseasonably warm temperatures.

Calmness turned to chaos in just moments, however, as the ghostly image of "Drop Tine" appeared 200 yards away, trotting through the swale, his nose to the ground. It was 4:45 p.m. and well before dark (in that part of Canada). Being caught off guard, my mind was now suddenly a blur, my heart was pounding like a hammer mill, and my breathing was uncontrollable. I alerted my son to the buck's presence and began to set up for a shot.

Basic shooting skills were awash in a sea of buck fever. In real terms a novice at trophy whitetail hunting, my sense of shock was overwhelming. My estimated distance of 150 yards was actually 175 yards and, although my breathing was out of control, I still managed to settle the crosshairs of my scope behind the deer's shoulder. I was, of course, going to shoot under him. Sure enough, the 300-grain sabot—pushed by 90 grains of Pyrodex—fell harmlessly beneath the deer.

The buck stood there momentarily, looking for the source of the sound, then moved casually toward the bush line. By the time I recovered my senses and began fumbling to reload—spilling some powder and dropping the cap three times—the buck disappeared into the bush. The disappointment was bitter. In my anguish, it felt as if my stomach rose to consume my heart.

Twenty or 30 minutes later, I saw the buck for a fleeting moment before he vanished again into the still and dark woodlot. I tried firing a quick off-handed shot, but the brute never slowed. Light was failing by the time my brother joined my son and me in a brief search for any sign of a hit. We finally decided to resume searching the next day.

We spent more than four hours combing the area the next morning, and I was back to search for several more hours the following day. But we found nothing. My insides had been in knots for days as I tried rejecting the notion that I had missed my opportunity. I didn't want to be dreaming about that errant shot and of the drop-tined buck.

Eventually, I found solace in the fact that it had been a clean miss. But I still dreamed about the buck.

For the first time, I was beginning to seriously question whether this drop-tined bruiser might indeed be "Curly." The travel route was familiar, and I'd gotten a good look at a long, sweeping main beam on the right side. But how could "Curly" have grown such a huge drop in a single season?

Even on the last morning of the season, Dec. 6, the thought of old Drop Tine continued to haunt my waking thoughts. As I lie in bed that morning with a severe cold coming on, I debated the wisdom in rising for one last hunt.

Still, I forced myself out of bed. I would hunt a morning stand in an area away from the drop-tined buck, saving an evening stand in the hope for one last chance. A quick telephone call to the weather office, however, forced a change of plans. The wind was wrong for my original morning stand, but it was perfect for hunting the area in which Drop Tine might appear.

I made my decision, had a leisurely breakfast, then drove to where I would leave my vehicle. I was feeling better as I walked toward my stand. A refreshing and cleansing wind was in my face, and it was still dark. In a mysterious way, I felt the pressures of having missed a once-in-a-lifetime opportunity begin to ease. I was reveling in each moment of the pre-dawn light as if I were in a trance.

When I stopped to glass the familiar pea field, I saw three does. I slipped in behind a round bale and watched for a time,

The buck has a near perfect frame, but the second growth on the left antler adds close to 50 inches of abnormal points. The rack scored 206⅞ (irregular) by BTR standards.

then stalked the deer cautiously, using the perimeter of the bush as cover. At less than 30 yards, I scanned the deer again. They sensed something amiss after several moments had passed, and moved away through the field to the west and out of sight.

That's when I picked up three more does, beyond the fence line in the alfalfa field. Once again I moved within closer range, using a Saskatoon berry bush for cover. As I observed, the does continued to browse on the second-growth alfalfa.

Glassing beyond them and down the fence line to the south, I focused on movement at 300 yards. This was a buck . . . This was, unbelievably and unmistakably, "Drop Tine." My senses once again flooded with emotion!

While struggling to contain and focus those effusions of adrenaline, I felt at the same time a keen sense of destiny. This buck and I seemed inextricably woven into a two-year-old and unfolding drama. My heart was again attempting to rupture my chest walls and my breathing was erratic, but this time my mind was clear.

27

Family Farm Bonanza

Hunter: Mark Moen
BTR Score: 127 5/8
Date Taken: Nov. 15, 1995
Typical; Compound Bow

Mark Moen has been hunting his family's 350-acre Iowa farm since he was a teenager. Even though it is just 12 miles from Des Moines, the largest city in the state, Mark regularly sees bucks here in the 120- to 140-class while bowhunting and scouting. The problem, of course, is that these bucks see a great deal of pressure from other hunters in the area and can be quite spooky.

Mark Moen with a bow-harvested buck that scored 127⅝ (typical) in the BTR system in 1995.

In 1995, Mark had a banner year of hunting by anyone's standards, taking two of the six bucks he's put in the Buckmasters record book within a month of each other. Extensive preseason scouting had shown him numerous scrapes and rubs in the area, which was a combination of river bottoms, hardwood ridges, and agricultural fields. He decided to hang two stands between a soybean field and pasture land overlooking the intersection of three well-traveled deer trails, one on top of a nearby ridge and the other below it. This was a tremendous hotspot for deer, as indicated by the amount of sign in the area, and Mark adjusted to hunt either stand depending on prevailing wind, time of day, and other conditions.

After taking a 144⅖-point buck from the ridge stand in October during muzzleloader season, Mark figured he'd probably taken his only trophy for the year. But hunting fever ran

Mark got off to a good start in 1995 during the blackpowder season in Iowa with this impressive buck—one of the two record-buck trophies he took that year.

strong in his blood and he was back in November to have a try with his bow from the bottom stand.

The stand was 30 yards back from the trail, and the only problem with this otherwise excellent spot, according to Mark, is that the wind is usually against you. It is predominantly out of the northwest and carries your scent into the nearby bedding areas.

He'd already hunted this stand a few times during that season and had chosen to pass on several worthy bucks—something every hunter must force himself to do if he wants to consistently harvest trophies. On the afternoon he chose to hunt, during the rut in November, it was a calm, clear day, around 35 degrees with no strong wind, a good omen. He arrived at the stand at around 1:30 and placed a few drops of estrus doe urine along the edge of the woods 20 yards away. He was in for a long wait.

After a slow afternoon without a single deer sighting, Mark's thoughts were beginning to drift toward dinner in a warm house as the sun sank toward the horizon.

Those thoughts quickly evaporated as a doe suddenly exploded from the woods behind the stand, with a 6-point and an 8-point buck hot on her trail. The three deer ran past the stand and into the woods on the adjoining ridge. Completely alert again, Mark spotted another larger buck head into the woods around 60 yards away from where the first deer had entered, obviously working his way up to the doe and young bucks.

Mark tried his grunt call a few times, but the bucks were too hot on the trail of the doe to break off now. With only around 10 minutes of legal shooting light left, the doe trotted down off the ridge and passed the stand again at around 20 yards. Mark geared up for a shot, as he knew the bucks would be right on her tail.

Twice he drew back on the largest buck and each time the buck moved suddenly, sprinting towards a smaller buck to drive it away and forcing Mark to hold the shot. Eventually, the buck stopped between the two smaller bucks, checking the wind for his doe and checking out the scent Mark had placed earlier. Mark took this opportunity to again come to full draw, centering the 30-yard pin just behind the buck's shoulder. He released his arrow and the buck bounded away.

With all of the excitement and only a few minutes of shooting time left, he immediately climbed down from his stand and ran back to the house to recruit his dad's tracking help. They arrived back an hour later and took up the trail. It was a sparse blood trail, but with persistence they found the buck only 40 yards from the stand. He was an 11-point typical with a BTR score of $127\tfrac{5}{8}$. It had been quite a season.

28

Monster of Muscatatuck

By John Trout, Jr.

Hunter: Dean Stallion
BTR Score: 176 5/8
Date Taken: Dec. 6, 1985
Irregular; Blackpowder Rifle

Few deer hunters would expect to find monstrous bucks roaming public lands. Most state- or federally-owned tracts are managed for quantity, not quality, because users generally prefer venison to antlers. But in a rare occurrence in 1985, Dean Stallion of Newburgh, Indiana, collected both—proof that you should never say never.

Most deer hunters would be surprised to find monster bucks like this one on public land. Dean Stallion took it with a muzzleloader.

Stallion was participating in a random draw hunt at the Muscatatuck National Wildlife Refuge in southern Indiana, an area comprised largely of rich bottomland. State officials decided in the early 1980s to schedule a primitive weapons hunt there to stabilize a growing deer herd. The hunt was open to carriers of both blackpowder rifles and bows.

Like other participants who were drawn for the third day's hunt with a muzzleloader, Stallion had high hopes of getting an opportunity to bring home one of the refuge's mature bucks.

Since he lived only three hours from the tract, Stallion took advantage of the scouting opportunities before his hunt day. He also met an individual who lived close to the refuge. The man said he had seen a bachelor group of bucks, and one of them was exceptional.

Before the Dec. 6 hunt, Stallion spent a lot of time looking for signs of the big buck along a creek bordering a swamp in the general area where the buck had been spotted. He was amazed at the amount of deer sign he found in the bottom, and he even saw the huge buck twice, figuring it for a heavy 8-pointer. He thought "8" when he saw three exceptional points on each beam. He wondered if it was the same buck that the local man had seen.

Stallion returned to that creek on the day of the hunt and climbed into a stand before dawn. He assumed that the half-mile-long swamp would be a safe haven for whitetails because few hunters ventured there.

That morning, he saw a few does and small bucks, but Stallion did not see the 8-pointer that had haunted his dreams. He later left the stand and returned to his vehicle to see if his partners needed help.

Around lunchtime, Stallion approached the same swamp from a different direction. He sat against the base of a tree to rest, planning to hang his stand about four hours before dusk. This would allow him to finish the day on alert and to perhaps get a last-minute crack at one of the refuge's reputed monsters. He would never get an opportunity to climb a tree.

"I figured I would sit there for an hour or so before setting up my stand," he said. "But as soon as I got into the area, there were deer coming in around me continuously. Some were feeding and others were just passing by. As it turned out, I never got a chance to get up in the stand."

After staying put for nearly an hour, Stallion spotted a group of several does and a few small bucks. But one buck stood out from the others. Stallion claims he would have gladly shot the trophy-class deer, yet another huge buck bringing up

This buck's unusual rack scored 176⅝ (irregular) in the Buckmasters scoring system.

the rear distracted him. It was the 8-pointer he'd seen while scouting.

"When I first saw him, he was quartering to me," he said. "At 60 yards, I thought he had to be the big 8-pointer." In less than a heartbeat, Stallion shouldered his one-shot muzzleloader as the buck stopped momentarily before crossing through an opening. By that time, Stallion's sights were falling over the buck's shoulder. He squeezed the trigger.

Stallion still remembers the cloud of smoke that blocked his view. In fact, the anxious hunter had to move away from the smoke to get a better look. Deer were running in every direction, including the buck—favoring his left front leg. The hunter attempted to reload the blackpowder gun, but the deer had disappeared before he could do it. A loud crash a short distance away led him to believe that the buck had fallen.

In less time than it takes to tell, Stallion moved forward and picked up a blood trail. He followed the red stuff for about 40 yards before tying a white handkerchief to a tree limb to mark the spot. He also veered away from the blood trail as he circled the area to look for the downed deer. This almost proved disastrous.

Instead of finding the deer, Stallion found himself turned around and unsure of which way to go. In fact, he came across a blood trail that he followed for a short distance, only to realize that the trail was from another deer that someone else had shot earlier in the day.

After about 40 minutes of panic, Stallion found himself back in the general area where he shot the buck. He was happy to see the white hanky. However, as he neared the makeshift marker, he spotted what he believed to be the exposed roots of a large tree. This was another welcome sight. Instead of a root, it was the buck of his dreams.

When the elated hunter got to the animal, he nervously examined its huge antlers. Stallion had thought the buck was a big 8-pointer because of the three long tines that were visible on both beams. But upon closer examination, he saw that the buck actually carried 17 scorable points.

The buck scored 176⅝ irregular in BTR's blackpowder category. However, the most fascinating feature may be the buck's moose-like antlers—the distinguishing characteristic that told him that it was the same deer he'd seen earlier. Incidentally, the buck had more than enough body weight to pack around those massive antlers. Its field-dressed weight was 191 pounds.

Stallion, a seasoned taxidermist, first did a life-sized mount of the buck. Today, however, the Muscatatuck monster resides as a shoulder mount atop a pedestal at American Taxidermy in Boonville, Indiana.

29

Home Field Advantage

**Hunter: Wesley Holm
BTR Score: 152 1/8
Date Taken: Nov. 6, 2000
Perfect; Compound Bow**

Wesley Holm has seen a lot of bucks cross his 14-acre property in Illinois since he purchased the land in 1966. He's taken 11 trophy-caliber deer here, including 5 bow-killed bucks registered in the Buckmasters record books, and he has allowed other hunters to have a try as well. He's seen as many as 56 deer pass through in a single day. The land is surrounded by 800 acres of strip-mine timber and has three established, well-traveled

Wesley Holm took this trophy buck, along with four others he's put in the record books, on a small piece of property he knows well.

deer trails traversing it. It is a piece of land Holm has come to know intimately, in all seasons. This knowledge has taught him when and how to take large bucks here virtually every year. He wears camouflaged clothing, but doesn't worry much about odor control or cover or attractor scents. Instead, he relies on the wind direction to know when hunting his stand—the only one he hunts from all season—will prove successful.

    The deer tend to move east through his property in the morning as they return from feeding in nearby grainfields, so a west, southwest, or south wind bodes well for morning hunts. In the afternoon, when the deer are moving back to feed, an east, northeast, or southeast wind works well. Using the same stand for 37 years has allowed him to watch how generations of deer have reacted to various conditions, and Wesley has come to know their territory better than the deer themselves. Every time he plays the wind right, he is sure to see a few animals.

But whitetails being whitetails, there are always a few surprises left in store. In early November 2000, Wesley decided to spend a day on his stand despite the fact that a 35- to 40-mph wind was howling through the trees. It was during the rut, of course, when a fevered buck may do just about anything, so he'd decided it was worth a shot. It was also an off day for Wesley, who discovered that the cap had fallen off the Cobra sight on his compound bow, leaving him in the low light of early dawn on a cloudy and dark morning without a lighted sight. As he sat hunched against the wind—just three minutes into legal shooting time—he wondered what in the world had possessed him to try to hunt that morning.

He didn't have long to wonder, though, as those three minutes were all the time it took for a huge buck to materialize from exactly the least expected direction. Wesley turned to see the buck coming in with the stiff wind directly at his back. This was rare enough for a mature buck, but the high winds were also making Wesley's stand squeak—something that usually made cagey bucks disappear in a flash. He'd noticed over the years that does and younger bucks would often hesitate for a minute or two when they heard this type of noise, but he had never seen a mature buck remain for more than a second or two.

This buck was a veteran of many seasons, but for some reason he stood still for several minutes, unable to smell Wesley without the help of the wind and evidently not spooked by the noise of the stand. Finally, he turned his head to look around and Wesley was able to grab his bow from the bow hanger, nock an arrow, and come to full draw. The buck took two steps and Wesley hit the release, sending the shaft right through his vitals within a comfortable shooting range.

The buck took off for the protective timber of the strip mine, and Wesley climbed down to examine the area around where he'd shot the buck. He found around 12 inches of his arrow snapped off with the vanes still attached and covered with blood, although there was no other blood on the ground. After he called his son to come help drag the buck out, he came back to follow in the direction the deer had taken.

The buck had gone down next to a deep ravine not too far away. Luckily, his large rack became entangled in two small trees that kept him from dropping another 40 feet straight down the steep-sided gully. He was shot through both lungs, which had evidently filled up with blood, as there was a large patch of blood that had been coughed up next to where the deer fell.

As Wesley Holm can attest, it doesn't matter how much you know about whitetails, their behavior will still surprise you from time to time. In this case, it turned out to be a most pleasant surprise.

30

Missouri 19-Pointer: Worth the Wait

Hunter: Gary J. Childress
BTR Score: 197 2/8
Date Taken: Nov. 18, 1998
Semi-Irregular; Rifle

Several years ago, I promised myself that I would not shoot a buck unless it was bigger than the mounts on my wall. Since I had three 130-class whitetails at home, I was looking for a deer with a rack carrying 140 or more inches of antler. I let 14 bucks pass by in 1997 alone—four or five in the 120 class and one in the 130s. I filled my three tags with does to help the deer herd.

MISSOURI 19-POINTER: WORTH THE WAIT

Gary Childress poses with the impressive buck he was willing to wait five years to find. The buck scored 197 2/8 (semi-irregular).

The 1998 season marked the fifth since I had put a buck on the ground. And prior to Missouri's rifle opener that year, I had allowed four young bucks to keep on trucking.

I was cradling my rifle in my treestand when the firearms season opened. A little 8-pointer went by first thing that morning, but I barely paid him any attention. My thoughts were of the monstrous buck that I had jumped during bow season. I'd also found some huge rubs on the farm, one of them 26 inches in diameter, so I knew a big buck was out there somewhere. Around 8:30 a.m., I moved to another tree near a historic big buck escape route.

I hadn't been in the tree 10 minutes when I saw a buck—a shooter! But he never stopped running. He was way too big to take a chance of wounding him, so I chose not to shoot. That night, I learned that at least six other hunters had seen the big buck, and two of them had taken shots. The rut was in full swing. I believe the buck was caught out after daylight and was making a dash for his sanctuary when we all saw him.

The buck was seen again the following day at 9:30 a.m. with his tongue hanging out, but he caught the hunter by surprise. The deer was headed toward a bedding area on the farm. Some members of our group wanted to drive the area later that afternoon, but we kept with our policy against deer drives.

The fifth day of rifle season, a Wednesday, was hot and windy. I sat on stand for more than an hour. Although the hunting pressure was light that day, nothing was moving. I only heard four or five shots all morning. Eventually, I decided to still-hunt. The wind was out of the east, in my favor.

I drove to another spot, got out, and began circling a big wet bottom that had not been planted that year. It had grown up in foxtail and weeds. I was headed for the timber on the other side. Unknowingly, I walked within 150 yards of the bedded buck. He had to be watching me the whole time, never moving from his bed.

With the wind in my face, I started my slow walk along the tip of the wooded bluffs overlooking the bottom. It took me two hours to cover 150 to 200 yards.

After hearing a loud crack—like the sound of a limb breaking—60 yards away, I saw a huge buck loping off along the bottom of the bluff. I just stood there in awe. Then I noticed a brown spot in the same blowdown from which the buck had just busted. I threw my gun up and looked through my scope to see a doe. I just stood there and waited.

After about five minutes, the doe stood up and walked around the same way the buck had gone. When she got out of sight, I took off in her direction. I walked up the hill and down the other side, then up the next hill. When I crested the second hill, I saw the buck take a step. I threw up my .270 and shot him as he was looking at me from about 75 yards distant. Afterward, the buck took a couple of steps and vanished behind the next bluff.

I walked over to where I thought the buck would be lying, but there was no deer. I thought that I'd missed. But when I went to the exact spot where the buck had been standing, I found blood and followed it for 20 yards to the deer.

When I reached the buck, I counted points. I told myself, "Gary, you've finally become a real deer hunter!"

I later noticed a cut on the buck's belly where he had been grazed by one of those opening-morning bullets. Had the shot been an inch higher, he might have been fatally wounded.

The buck scored 197⅞—well worth the wait.

31
Land of the Giants

Hunter: Phil Kozak
BTR Score: 153; 192$\frac{3}{8}$
Dates Taken: Oct. 25, 2000;
Oct. 26, 2001
Regular: Compound Bow
Semi-Irregular: Compound Bow

It took five years for my buddy Fred Burgstahler to convince me that if you want the ultimate trophy whitetail, you should go to Alberta. Fred has been to Alberta many times before on rifle hunts, and did take a whopper buck grossing 185 inches. I myself had hunted Saskatchewan and British Columbia many times be-

Kozak with the 19-pointer he took on October 26, 2001.

fore for various game, but had never taken a whitetail over 170 inches.

In October 2000, Fred finally convinced me to go. Obviously, a land where the average mature white-tailed deer exceeds 150 inches is no doubt a hunter's paradise. Alberta is a very tough hunt, due to the enormous size of the fields in the southern part of the province. We all were warned by outfitter Percival McKinnon that a bowhunt would probably produce only a 25 percent chance for success in an area that is mainly rifle country. Needless to say those odds are not for the fainthearted, but we knew that if we were to take record-class deer, this was the place.

We had a very successful bowhunt with three of us scoring on very nice whitetails, not to mention the monsters we had seen just out of range. We called the area "Land of the Giants" due to the extremely large body sizes, 250 pounds plus, and the unusually large racks. After our return in October 2000, we immediately started to plan our next year's hunt. I had prepared all year for the October 2001 hunt, joining the summer and fall bow leagues at the Monksville Sportshop in West Milford, New Jersey, practicing out to eighty yards. I knew that if I could increase my shooting distance, it would increase my odds, and build confidence.

During our 3½ hour ride northeast from Edmonton to Glendon, I was noticing more and more of the white stuff on the ground. It was really exciting to see snow, and this would make it easier to find good hunting spots during our scheduled Sunday scouting mission. The Alberta pre-rut gets underway right around the 25th of October, just before the rifle season opens on November 1. Needless to say, hunting with the bow on dry ground in Alberta is difficult at best, as the deer are difficult to pattern, and you have to depend on early-season buck sign, of which there is little.

Sunday we were all up at 5 a.m. for a full day of scouting. Looking at all the 160 to 200-inch plus whitetails hanging on the wall the night before had built excitement in our group, like a bunch of kids the night before Christmas.

This hunt was particularly special, as my dad (Phil Sr.) and brother-in-law (George Monarque) had accompanied me. After a hearty breakfast, we put on a bunch of "klicks," (Canadian slang for kilometers), punching through thick bush and field edges. The areas were then chosen where we would settle in for the week's hunt.

I chose an area where Doug Percival had seen two 160-inch plus bucks the week prior to our arrival. The area was not particularly interesting to me as there was little to no buck sign, but plenty of tracks going in straight lines through a heavily wooded patch that encompassed approximately three to four wooded quarter sections. A quarter section is made up of approximately 160 acres. The area was surrounded by recently cut alfalfa, called stubble fields, with a river flanking the east side. Two of the fields, to the north and south remained stubble with the other field area plowed under.

The deer tracks seemed to be going in a direct north and south line through the center of the woodlot, making it easy to move east and west in hopes of intercepting deer moving back and forth between the two stubble fields.

On Monday, the first day of the hunt, I had seen a small 7-pointer with a doe at 8:00 a.m. followed by a nice symmetrical palmated 10-point, somewhere between the 145 to 155-inch-class. I took a shot at the 10-point missing and shooting low. I had assumed the buck at 30 yards; later to find out it was more like 44 yards to be exact. I wasn't upset with my miss and told this to the boys later that night in camp, it really wasn't what I was after. Tuesday morning brought me back to the same spot but all I saw was a bunch of trophy Canadian red squirrels.

Tuesday afternoon brought warmer weather with the thermometer touching the 38 degree mark, melting the top half inch of snow slightly by nightfall.

Tuesday provided no deer sightings, a depressing day at best. Wednesday morning I decided to move 150 yards down towards the river. I soon found myself in a poplar tree along an old overgrown logging trail, but with little cover.

I climbed to about eighteen feet and settled in the poplar for the morning hunt. Just at first light, able to see only 20 yards, I heard two deer creep by me at about 40 yards. The thermometer was just touching 20 degrees, making the slight snowmelt from Tuesday sound like Rice Krispies.

The deer had gone by me without a glimpse. At about 7:20 a.m. I heard what seemed to be a large buck whacking his rack on a tree 80 yards in front of me. My heart started to pound with excitement, and I quickly reached for my grunt call, in hopes of making the deer curious enough to come take a peek. As I grunted, the noise of the rack whacking a tree seemed to get more aggressive, as the sound echoed through the deafening quietness of the Alberta woods.

No luck, so I reached for my rattling bag and made a tickle of the horns; again no luck. The woods became quiet and I decided to get down around 11:00 a.m. to go have a look around. I noticed that all the deer tracks went north and south and the closer I got to the river and to this large spruce forest, the more and bigger tracks I was seeing. I also noticed that the deer seemed to hook slightly toward the river, once in the spruce forest, a quarter section I would not venture into, as it looked like the main bedding area.

During my mini scouting adventure, I found a perfect tree for the following morning's hunt, a good-size poplar nestled tight against a big spruce. But this wouldn't provide a good evening spot so I decided to climb back up the same poplar I had been hunting in the morning. At an hour before dark, I saw the same 7-pointer from Monday and three does.

That evening, back at camp, I explained my hunt with great excitement, from the sounds of a giant buck smacking trees earlier that day. I was eager to try out my new-found spot the following morning. Thursday morning the thermometer had plummeted to a bone-chilling 17 degrees with a slight wind blowing from the northeast, making it feel like below zero.

I had some problems that morning, with my feet sticking to the aluminum Loggy Bayou treestand, making it difficult to move without the treestand popping and pinging, frustrating to any bowhunter . . . "must get close enough to kill."

At about 8:30 a.m., four bucks walked right under my stand making their way out into a 60 by 100 yard brushy meadow out in front of me.

Three 8-pointers and a really nice 6-pointer with no brow tines stopped at about 40 yards and decided to put on a morning show. They all started a semifriendly sparring match, which I thought was pretty neat. I figured if there were any giants around, this would be sure to bring them in. Again, no luck. At this point I was feeling I was in the "land of the mutants," with no big-buck sign, no scrapes, and a bunch of small bucks, but that sound of a huge buck whacking his rack in the same area on Wednesday kept going through my mind.

I kept thinking to myself "what was that and how big?" Thursday afternoon I needed a change of scenery, so I hunted with my dad in an evening spot he'd been hunting littered with giant buck sign. More than 20 table-sized scrapes and 15 giant buck rubs within a 150-yard area. Seeing all this sign, I started doubting the area I was hunting.

The Thursday evening hunt provided me a "second wind" in hopes of scoring on a giant. But again, no luck. Thursday night I started double guessing my missed shot at the 10-pointer on Monday. Maybe that was my one and only opportunity, as there was only Friday and a half day of Saturday left to hunt.

I started preparing myself mentally to go home empty-handed. Kept thinking, "it ain't over till it's over." I figured it was time to break out the artillery; with only one full day left to the hunt, what did I have to lose. I'm one of the guys who keep the scent companies in business, a "scent junkie." Over my 30 years of hunting, I have used all types of scents and got my chops busted last year by the owners Dale & Doug. They called my scents "flames & thunderbolts." You know, when you put down the scents the skies open up and the deer come runnin'. I am a true believer in scents.

It doesn't work all the time, but if you put your time in the woods to see the results, you'll be a believer too. I've been experimenting with pre-season scents for the past few years and found that Bob Kirschner's "Curiosity" in the pre-rut and James Valley "Doe in Estrus" gel scent in the rut produces amazing results on bucks if they hit the scent trail. I've seen bucks actually follow the scent trail like a hound dog, rolling their upper lips to get a better whiff. Over the last three years, I can attribute the use of these scents to three successful kills, including my buck taken last October in Alberta. Friday led me back to my perfect tree in the "area of the mutants." I used the "Curiosity" scent from three known deer runs to my stand sight.

I just sprayed it directly from the bottle to the ground, to the area I wished the bucks to walk if they hit the scent trail. I carried in an extra camo sweatshirt for the bottom of my aluminum Loggy so my feet wouldn't stick, in hopes of stopping the popping and pinging of my treestand. The sweatshirt worked out nicely, my feet were now only freezing to the sweatshirt, but it made for much quieter movement. I also brought my dad and placed him where I had seen the two bucks on Monday, as he wasn't seeing any bucks in his area, littered with unimaginable monster buck sign.

They must have been making the sign at night. We had brought in Motorola 10X radios as a safety item, due to my dad having a problem with the cold weather. As we entered the woods, we decided we would try to contact each other every half hour starting at 8:30 a.m. I got nestled in at about 6:50 a.m., another cold morning around 17 degrees with an ever so slight thermal current making your breath seem to linger for hours, like a puffy white cloud after you exhaled.

I broke off two small pieces of the spruce branch and doused some of my James Valley doe estrus gel and threw the small pieces 10 yards out to my left. I got all my accessories organized and had a seat and waited for first light.

At 7:10 a.m. I heard a deer walking up from behind me. First thoughts were . . . "this has got to be one of the mutants I've been seeing all week." I didn't even stand up from my seat. I would hear three to four steps punching through the ice crusted snow, then a long pause, which seemed to be in 5-minute intervals. I peeked around the spruce I was against, peeking through the bare spots of the frost-covered spruce branches, to where the sound was coming from, but couldn't see anything. I started to think, "maybe it's a coyote or something?"

Slowly the movement grew near, still no sighting. I decided to rise slowly off my seat to get a better look. As I peered through the frost-covered branches of the spruce tree, I couldn't believe my eyes. At 40 yards stood a buck with points all over the place! I started losing my composure, my heartbeat soared, and my knees started to shake slightly. There he stood like a frozen statue, my dream buck. "What's his next move?" I thought to myself. Talking to myself, and it wasn't in these exact words, as you can imagine . . . "don't foul this up" . . . "you hunted for over 30 years for this opportunity" . . . "calm down" . . . these thoughts raced through my head.

As the buck moved closer he started to hook to my right side. With my back to him, being a right-hand shooter, I needed to turn to my right for the shot. When he reached 30 yards, I decided it was time for me to get into position for a straight-down shot to my right. As I moved my left foot in slow motion to my right and placed it down, my tree stand made a "tink" sound. Apparently, there was some melted snow that had frozen up between my sweatshirt and treestand. He came to an immediate halt, snapped his head up looking beyond the tree I was standing in. My heart sank to my stomach, and the adrenaline rush was gone. I thought all my chances of him were lost.

The buck stood frozen in time, not moving a muscle. I did the same. The standoff lasted a gut-wrenching 15 minutes or more, until he felt safe enough to make a move. He cautiously moved closer to my tree, burying his head in the branches of the spruce below me, interested to see what made that unearthly sound. The heart rate started to rise again as I peered down through the iced spruce branches watching his rack almost touch the poplar I was in, at the same time trying not to start counting points.

"Must keep focused" . . . "he's going to come to my right" . . . "I'll have to wait until he passes me to shoot" . . . I thought to myself. With that, the buck stepped backwards out from the spruce tree.

"He either scented me or possibly smells the scent I put out" . . . I thought to myself. The buck now decided to move to the left side of the tree to my surprise, and continued a nonstop strut with his nose to the ground! I'm now in position to make a right-sided shot, and the buck walks to the left, through my 10-yard shooting lane and then heads away to my left towards the spruce forest. I pivot my left foot to the left at the same time, in one single motion, coming to a full draw. I have to extend out to the outer edge of my treestand to shoot around a tree that's between the buck and me.

He's about 20 yards, walking dead away, I aim for the center of his back and let it rip. My 72-pound Martin bow sends my Game Tracker carbon arrow with a Thunderhead 100 at 276 feet per second into the center of his back, driving forward into the chest cavity, burying the arrow to the fletching.

Like slow motion, the buck makes a hard left leap and bounds out of sight into the spruce forest, crashing back to my

The 10-pointer shot by the author on Oct. 25, 2000.

left, then comes bounding out 40 yards behind me, going straight away from where I first saw him appear. I look at my watch, it's 8:10 a.m., I take a huge deep breath and say what a buck. As I see him for the last time, I notice the giant spread from the back view and I mark the last spot I saw him vividly in my mind.

At 8:25 a.m. I turn my Motorola radio on, at 8:35 a.m. I hear the faint whisper of my dad calling. I told my dad I had just shot a really nice buck, and he decided to cut his hunt short, and to give him 20 minutes to get down to me. I figured that my dad was like a Popsicle, keeping in mind it's 17 degrees.

During this 20-minute period, I hear a deer walking back through the spruce forest below towards the river. I think to myself, "that's my buck, he's still alive" and get another arrow ready. The deer continues past me just out of my sight. I figure my shot may have caught just shoulder meat and nothing vital, panic starts to set in. I'm sure all you hunters can attest to a panic attack.

Your mind has its way of playing those tricks on you until your eyes finally set in on the buck motionless on the ground. That's when the relief and reality really sets in. Until then, it's the sweats and nailbiting. My dad shows up 20 minutes later, walking within 20 yards and not seeing me. A quick "Psssst" gets his startled attention. I whisper and point with my arrow, like a pointer stick, to where the buck was standing. My dad couldn't believe how close he was, shaking his head in amazement. I lowered my bow, then descended from the tree like a fireman on a pole. I walked directly to where I had seen the buck last and followed the huge tracks with my dad for about 50 yards, not expecting to find blood right away due to the high back shot. No blood!

I started getting nervous and that empty feeling in my stomach. We followed the tracks a bit more and the deer hooked back just below me in the spruce forest, confirming the deer I had heard just before my dad arrived. My dad suggested we go back to the spot where I had shot him and pick up the tracks from there. My dad figured we might find the arrow or something that would indicate the type of hit. We followed the tracks about 35 yards from where I had taken the shot and my dad points ahead to where he had stumbled, blowing the dirt from the spruce forest floor on top of the snow.

My dad said . . . "Philly, he's hurt, looks like he stumbled here." With our bodies hunched over focused on the tracks, we went 35 yards further, looked up, and there he lay behind a blown-down spruce tree. Relief overwhelmed my body followed by an excitement I can't even explain.

I went to the deer and pulled out my arrow, it was a perfect liver and lung shot, and the buck only went 70 yards. We admired the rack and body size and started counting . . . "he's 15 points!" . . . counting again . . . "no . . . he's 17 points!" My dad says "Philly, did you count the drop tines?" Grand total 19 points! We both couldn't believe the rack on this buck. Later, it weighed in at 278 pounds and well over 300 on the hoof!

We both laughed and remembered a similar situation, twenty some years ago in Maine, when my dad had taken a really big buck.

We left the buck covered up and started heading out. At 11:00 a.m., Doug mics up with me on the radio, and I advise him to go back to camp to get a quad, that we have a monster down. Doug eagerly arrived back at the hunting sight about an hour later, excited to see the buck, "Thank God for quads!" If we had to drag this brute we'd need an ambulance to get us out. Arriving at the buck, Doug started hooting and hollering, giving the high fives. He was just as excited as I was.

Although the buck's rack is built on a typical 165-inch frame, the enormous amount of scorable points skyrockets the Pope & Young score into the high 190s. The required 60-day drying period passed, and the buck officially scored 192⅜ gross and nets 190⅝. A current copy of the Alberta record book will unveil the final record standings.

My dad did give the other buck a try on Saturday morning with no luck. I'm sure glad my dad was there to see me take my trophy buck. Like twenty-some years ago in Maine, when my dad had taken his nice buck, I saw the same excitement in his eyes and I was there to share in his moment of success. He's in his 60s now, has old-age ailments, and says this is probably his last hunt. I will probably never top this buck of a lifetime, grossing over 190, but more so with 19 points and double drop tines, but you never know what lurks in the big woods of Alberta . . . it's the "Land of the Giants."